MAKE IT Mighty Ugly

MAKE IT Mighty Ugly

EXERCISES & ADVICE FOR GETTING CREATIVE EVEN WHEN IT AIN'T PRETTY

KIM PIPER WERKER

SASQUATCH BOOKS
SEATTLE

Printed in ther United States of America

Published by Sasquatch Books

18 17 16 15 14   9 8 7 6 5 4 3 2 1

Editor: Gary Luke
Project editor: Michelle Hope Anderson
Art director: Anna Goldstein
Illustrations: Kate Bingaman-Burt
Design: Joyce Hwang
Copy editor: Rebecca Brinson

Library of Congress Cataloging-in-Publication Data
is available.

ISBN: 978-1-57061-914-4

Sasquatch Books
1904 Third Avenue, Suite 710
Seattle, WA 98101
(206) 467-4300
www.sasquatchbooks.com
custserv@sasquatchbooks.com

Certified Chain of Custody
SUSTAINABLE Promoting Sustainable Forestry
FORESTRY
INITIATIVE www.sfiprogram.org
SFI-01268

SFI label applies to the text stock

To Owen

Contents

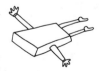

Introduction

You could fill a very big boat with books like this one, about creativity and overcoming creative challenges. If that boat were to start taking on water, you might be able to find among those books enough titles worthy of sharing space on your lifeboat and still have enough room to save some of your travel companions from a watery death. Those books are smart and wonderful. The rest, though. Well. It's possible part of the reason I'm writing this book at all is because the rest of those books seem to share a couple of troubling qualities that defeat the purpose of encouraging creativity and new habits. Those useless qualities are *cheerleading* and *hand-waving*. Nothing makes me want books to drown more than cheerleading and hand-waving.

When you're running a race and you get to the point where you feel like dying would be a relief, people shouting, "You can do it! You rock!" can be a very effective motivator. But when you're reading a book, there's just got to be more. *Why? Why do I rock? How do* you *know I can do it?* When the author then rolls in the egomaniacal hand-waving of, "Just do what I did and you'll be as blissfully happy all the time and filthy rich, like I am!" or the even less helpful, "Just do the work!" it's time to just gently set the book back on the shelf and walk away.

Don't get me wrong. I appreciate enthusiastic encouragement, I really do. What I don't believe, though, is that a book that's 90 percent cheerleading and 10 percent vague advice is actually useful. And I don't want to live my life like other people, anyway; I want to live my life like me. I bet you want to live your life like you, too.

So here's how things are going to go with this book.

1. We're going to assume I believe you can do it—whatever it is—and we're going to leave it at that. If you start envisioning me waving pom-poms as you read, send me an e-mail and tell me I've done it wrong.

2. There's work you need to do (I do the same work, so don't think I'm just pointing at you from afar here). The work does not consist of, "Follow these steps that *I* took so you can achieve tremendous success and make several dozen masterpieces every week! Listen to these vague platitudes about how you should develop a routine like mine and eat a special kind of diet like mine and get a pet like mine!" No. I'm going to tell you about my experience, not because I think there's anything in the details that can or should be copied or emulated, but because I want you to know that you're not alone in wanting some help; that you're not alone in struggling, in feeling confused or lost, in being blocked, in feeling you're not creative (but secretly wishing you were).

This *knowing you're not alone* part? Don't underestimate the power of that. (**SPOILER ALERT:** If you get nothing from this book other than the knowledge that you're not alone in your creative struggles, I'm going to call it a win, because there's so much you can do with that knowledge. I don't need to be a part of it; do with it what you will, and I hope what you do makes you happy and helps you work through the struggles to the good stuff.)

I'm going to tell you about my own experience because it's the story I have to tell. I created Mighty Ugly in an effort to help myself and other people both fight and embrace creative demons; I have demons, you have demons, we all have them. I've spent quite a lot of time getting to know mine, and that I win more battles against them than I lose these days is possibly my crowning achievement. But more than that, my acceptance that my demons will never, ever fully die—that's the thing that gets me out of bed in the morning. That there is no *end* in the grand creative adventure; it's an adventure we get to enjoy forever and ever.

So that's it. Don't trust me because I'm a celebrity (I'm not). Don't trust me because I've gotten rich (I haven't; I'm probably watching *Buffy* and knitting in my pajamas and eating nachos while you read this). Don't trust me because I have credentials and awards that appease your concern that I'm full of crap (I don't; Google won't unearth much of anything beyond lots of blogging and a few books I've written and some photos of my dog and crafts). Trust me because I'm being honest with you about the ups and downs, and because I think we should have coffee someday and talk about it all. Or, you know what? Be a skeptic. Don't trust me at all unless you feel like it.

EMBRACING THE DARK SIDE

This book is not about *killing* your creative demons. Creative demons—the dark side of creativity—are important. Like the bacteria in your gut that help you digest your food, your demons keep your creative engines purring. Without them, you'd be stuck making stuff from a place of benign blandness—everything would be rainbows and unicorns and paint-by-number and sunflowers after a summer rain. Your demons, mean and challenging as they may be, are what make your experiences unique and your creations meaningful.

We will fight our demons, yes, but we'll do it knowing that they never die beyond a state of *mostly dead*. That's OK. Part of getting past the demons to the creativity and the making of stuff is accepting that the demons exist and learning to cope with them. People who have no demons are robots. Cool as robots are, people are cooler.

Right. Since I already said I'm not a fan of you-can-do-itism, these pages contain, in equal(ish) measure, tales of my own battles in hopes you might relate to them in ways that will help you with your own; exercises that are designed more to give you something concrete to try than to be used as a cure-all; wise words and anecdotes from people who are not me, because my stories can get old real fast and theirs are different and wonderful; and tips and notes about other places to seek out information and inspiration for your continuing adventures. As I said, this book is but one amongst dozens, if not hundreds, on this topic, many of which are filled with ace ideas that transcend vague cheering (there's a bibliography at the end of the book for you to mine when you're so inclined). And the internet! Filled with brilliance.

Here's another thing: This book is **YOURS**. Mark it up, fold down the pages, cut things out. It is not precious. It is, in fact, meant to be **USED.***

FAILURE AS FOUNDATION

J.K. Rowling, author of the *Harry Potter* books, delivered the commencement address at Harvard in 2008. It's a moving, inspiring speech about the experiences that led her to create one of the most iconic stories of our time. In addition to explaining why imagination is such an important human trait for the empathy it enables, she talked about how failing miserably in her twenties allowed her to achieve such greatness later on:

> **"I was set free because my greatest fear had been realized, and I was still alive . . . and I had an old typewriter and a big idea. And so rock bottom became the solid foundation on which I rebuilt my life."**

----

* Unless you borrowed it from a friend or the library, in which case I recommend the photocopier for choice sections.

Which is not to imply that we must hit rock bottom before we're ready to succeed. Nor should we believe that our success should be defined by someone else's achievement. But I do mean to imply that knowing we can survive the realization of our worst creative fears can be a profoundly empowering experience. In fact, we're going to *seek out* those fears so we can stare them down and get on with the making of stuff already.

HOW TO MAKE THE MOST OF THIS BOOK

We all struggle with our creativity. All of us. My biggest struggles have been with needing things that are different from what "normal" people need and not being able to do what "normal" people do; with valuing creative satisfaction in my work more than the salary I earn; with getting bored very, very quickly; with not handling that boredom well; with being a crafty self-saboteur; with feeling electric when I start a big project and like I'm about to die when I'm nearly done with it; with feeling physically ill when my work doesn't afford me independence and flexibility.

For lots of people, the root of creative struggle is fear of failure, whether that failure is defined as making something ugly (not on purpose), or not making enough money to pay their rent, or having someone criticize or reject their work. For some, it's perfectionism—not being able to let their work go until it's absolutely perfect, which of course it will never be. For some, it's crushing self-doubt. For most of us, at one time or another, it's block. For many of us, it's feeling like a freak for some reason or another.

This book is divided into three parts. **PART ONE: NAME THE DEMONS** is the one that will hopefully make you the most uncomfortable (that's right, this whole book might make you uncomfortable at times—discomfort is what will help the most). This part is where we'll look very closely at the ugly side of creativity. It's here that we'll explore and examine the fears, doubts, panics, and stresses that haunt us, even when we try to pretend they don't exist. We're going to name these creative demons. And we're going to spend a lot of time listening to the voice in each of our heads that makes us miserable. You know the one—it tells you your ideas aren't any good, that no one will care about what you do or make, that you're not good enough, that you're not qualified, and that you're going to fail. (Yes, everyone who's ever wanted to make or achieve anything has that stupid voice in their head.) We're going to be the bigger person, and at the same time that we tell that voice to quiet down, we're going to make friends with it (or, well, at least we'll try to be frenemies). I share some of my own creative struggles here, and walk you through taking a good, long look at yours.

They will be different, my struggles and yours. If we were all the same, the world would be a sad, boring place, indeed. *You're not alone.* That's the point. For every way you think you're not creative or talented or cool or whatever, there's someone else out there who thinks the same thing. And you're both wrong.

The rest of the book is about establishing a habit of creative exploration—first about just getting off your butt to make anything at all, and then about making an effort to find your favorite thing (or things) and doing it (or them) as much as you can. You may be an avid crafter or artist just looking for new ways to stay on track or break out of a rut, or you may be like I was not very long ago—feeling desperate for some sort of creative outlet but convinced you're not creative at all. Maybe you'll get the most out of the book if you read it all in one go, doing every exercise until you get to the end; maybe you'll get more if you read it and do the exercises in bits and pieces over days and months and years. There's no right or wrong way to do it; just do it.

PART TWO: MAKE STUFF is about getting (back) in touch with your creativity. This section is about casting a wide net so you can catch something interesting—something that sparks your imagination, that stirs your creative insides. I wrote this section as much for people who have always believed they're *not* creative as for people who have lost touch with their creativity or just need a little nudge. We're going to challenge ourselves and hopefully have some fun, all with the goal of bringing some wonder and levity (back) into our lives, so we can take the leap into making stuff instead of just thinking about making stuff.

PART THREE: KEEP ON MAKING STUFF is about taking the foundations we laid in Part Two and building a creative life on top—it's about deliberately suffusing our lives with creative pursuits that make us feel happy and satisfied. Here, we examine the environment we live in and explore how we can adapt it to fit our creative needs. We revisit the voice in our head we got to know in Part One, and we start talking back to it so it quiets down and lets us make stuff in peace. We take a look at how we spend our time, what makes us happy and what makes us feel drained, and we explore ways we can make more time for creative projects. We also pay attention to maintaining and sustaining our creative momentum once we get going. We'll look at ways to keep ourselves full of inspiration, how to handle ruts and blocks, and in general how to keep our creative gears oiled and aligned. (Does one align gears? I really need to learn more about mechanics. I trust you get my drift.)

Each part includes exercises to help you figure out what's going on in the back of your mind: Which demons are holding you back and why, what can you do about it, and how can you embrace them to fuel your creativity? What is your ugly voice saying and why, and how can you quiet it? What are your dreams, what do you strive to accomplish, how can you achieve it, and what can you do to grow into your creative skin so you can feel complete and make stuff?

AN IMPORTANT NOTE

I use *ugly* both literally and metaphorically. It should be obvious which is which in the context of what you're reading. For most of the book, I use the term as a metaphor for anything that's less than pleasant, from mild squirmy feelings to abject failure. *Ugly* is the blanket term for the vital parts of creativity we like to pretend don't exist—fear of failure or judgment, block, perfectionism, procrastination, self-doubt. By the end of this book, I hope you'll be far more intimately engaged with the ugly parts of your creative life. That intimacy is what will set you free.

Something compelled you to pick up this book. Whatever it is is unique to you, but I'm going to go ahead and assume that, broadly speaking, there's something nagging at you. There's a good chance you don't really know exactly what it is yet, and that's OK. This book is intended to be simple, straightforward, and enjoyable; hopefully it'll shake something loose that will help you work through that nagging feeling. Pick and choose exercises as you'd like, but be sure to do the ones that make you uncomfortable. Staying comfortable won't shake anything loose at all.

Whatever creative demons you're looking to battle, other people have been there, and I bet I've been there, too. Sometimes I've been wounded in fighting my demons, sometimes I've felt sure I wouldn't survive the fight, and in all cases I came out not only alive, but happier. It's your turn now. Take a deep breath. Sharpen your sword.

I MAKE UGLY THINGS ON PURPOSE.

I do it because I'm afraid to make ugly things *not* on purpose. I do it because I'm a self-saboteur. I do it when I'm stuck. I do it because I'm a big old fraud.

Don't get me wrong—I don't only make ugly things. I usually try hard to make any other kind of thing, really. Making ugly things on purpose helps me do that, though. It helps me feel unencumbered and able to go where my imagination wants to take me; it helps me feel comfortable taking risks, and it helps me muster the confidence to try to make not-ugly things.

I can get so laser-focused on making pretty things, successful things, that I inevitably end up in a tizzy. A downright frizzy-haired, bags-under-the-eyes, I'll-never-make-anything-again, I'd-better-get-a-day-job, I'm-going-to-burn-all-my-knitting-needles-and-notebooks-and-pipe-cleaners-and-fabric-and-thread, I-may-never-do-my-laundry-again downward spiral of angst and misery.

Making ugly things helps me keep it real. It forces me to shift my focus from the pressure to succeed to actually just making things. Making things makes me feel happy and capable, even when I struggle to do it right. Working materials with my hands is relaxing and challenging. And I admit it doesn't hurt that making stuff makes me feel pretty confident about surviving the zombie apocalypse. Or the nuclear winter (which, let's face it, is the more likely scenario [all due respect to the undead]).

Making ugly things reminds me to pay attention to the process of making, rather than obsessing about the product. It reminds me I've made mistakes and failed and will make more mistakes and fail again, and that I haven't died from it yet, and I won't die from it next time, so I'd better just keep on making things.

The whole idea of Mighty Ugly—a project I do with all sorts of people with the goal of embracing the dark parts of creativity so we stop holding ourselves back—is to take the uncomfortable parts of creative exploration and turn them upside down and inside out. To say, "Oh, you're afraid you'll crash and burn? Let's start out making what that spectacular failure will look like, then go from there." It's about pointing a finger at our fears and the things that make us uncomfortable when it comes to creativity and making things. These fears and discomforts are the feelings we force to the back of our minds, as if ignoring them will defuse their power over us.

Obviously, I don't need to tell you that ignoring them isn't an effective solution. You and I both know these things we ignore have a way of nagging at us, of keeping us awake at night, of screwing our insides up and just generally making us miserable. When ignored, the creative dark side festers and eventually, at seemingly random intervals, springs sneak attacks that can downright cripple us. Taking a long hard look at these fears and discomforts—stopping ourselves from pretending they don't exist—can help put an end to the sneak attacks and allow us to explore our creativity more freely.

This book is not about working *around* our creative demons, but about identifying and slaying them. It's a war without end, though, so don't get your hopes up about a quick fix that'll heal your creative soul overnight and set you on a path to unicorns and double rainbows. Demons procreate like bunnies on amphetamines, so what we'll do here is train for a lifelong quest to keep them at bay. But do note that nothing is as dire or scary as the first few battles. Whatever your goal—be it to fill an amorphous void, to make more space and time for creative experiences in your life, to seriously ramp up your commitment to making stuff—you'll feel better for fighting the fight.

Here in Part One, we're going to start at the very beginning by identifying your demons. They're different for all of us, so though I'll tell you about the forces that plague me, I've also asked some other people to share tales of their own battles. The goal is for you not only to realize, but to get comfortable with the knowledge that everyone—dude, **EVERYONE**—has demons that tell them they suck, that hold them back, that occasionally paralyze them or sucker punch them or make fun of their lopsided drawings. We all develop our own ways to fight back, and the ideas in this book are only a start.

The most important thing is that you do the work. No platitude will help you. No amount of rah-rah cheerleading will slay your demons for you. Platitudes and cheerleading may help get you through the thick of a battle, but you have to be the one to fight the fight.

ABOUT FEAR AND MIGHTY UGLY

I've worked in the crafts industry for a decade, and there has been one refrain I've encountered more than any other, one that remained a mystery to me for many years.

"I'M AFRAID TO TRY THAT."

I'd respond with a double take (yes, every time). "What now? It's yarn," I'd say. "It won't hurt you, and if you screw up, you can just unravel what you did and start again." I would be met most frequently by a blank stare, as if I clearly hadn't understood what they meant.

Later, I'd wave my arms and rant about my exasperation to other designers and writers and artists. They'd nod knowingly, and we'd remind each other that only some crafters design and innovate; most follow instructions. This is not a bad thing. Naturally, designing and inventing and innovating are not the only outlets for creativity. Improving upon or even just altering these designs by making decisions about colors, techniques, textures, riffing off what other people have done—all creative. And there's undeniable satisfaction to be found in relaxing into following someone else's instructions to the letter, step-by-step making something that didn't exist before.

Anyway, after my rant, I'd feel understood in my confusion and validated in my frustration that so many people—a huge number of people—prevent themselves from trying new things, even by making the smallest of alterations to what's already been made by someone else. It's not a phenomenon specific to yarn crafts, or crafts in general. People refuse to try all sorts of things, from dancing to cooking to drawing to tennis.

And I simply could not grasp what the big scary deal was, even though I heard the same thing over and over and over again, from all sorts of people, from all sorts of places.

WHAT'S TO FEAR?

Then I had an unusual experience that wasn't very unusual at all, and I started to get it.

One day in the mid-2000s, my friend Ian threw himself a birthday party. He filled his living room with scrap craft supplies, set up a couple of sewing machines, and covered the few remaining surfaces of his apartment with treats and drinks.

As a [insert serious-sounding voice here] Crafter, I was very excited for this party. This was my kind of social event. But it didn't turn out the way I'd planned. Not so fun, kind of uncomfortable.

I was overwhelmed by the variety of materials and realized I felt totally uncomfortable when I thought of making anything that wasn't crocheted or knitted. Then I became certain that someone would finally discover that I was a big old crafty fraud who wasn't actually creative and didn't know how to make anything and wasn't fun or worth inviting to birthday parties ever again.

After a drink or two, and feeling glum, I sat down next to a bag of fabric scraps and tried to disappear. Then I looked over at the bag and before I knew it I fell in love with some upholstery fabric. Hideous upholstery fabric. It was orange and green and white, and made me imagine the person who might choose to cover an entire sofa in it. People have since pointed out to me that if you glance at the fabric a certain way, it looks like brain pizza. I was truly in love with it. What must a room with that sofa have looked like, in its entirety? Surely something to behold. Despite my discomfort and the sad time I was having, I desperately wanted to make a doll from this awful fabric.

Only thing was, I only knew how to make stuff that was crocheted or knitted. I didn't know a thing about sewing dolls. I could barely sew a button, and artlessly at that.

I felt my chest tighten. *What will people think of me? They'll know I'm a fraud. I'd better set this fabric down. I'm not really crafty at all. Charlatan!*

I was, with sweaty palms and everything, **AFRAID**.

> In the spring of 2013, actor Mandy Patinkin was interviewed by Jian Ghomeshi on my favorite radio show, CBC's *Q*. I enjoy listening to actors, musicians, and artists talk about their work and the events in their lives that affect their creativity. Patinkin was profoundly honest about his relationship with fear, explaining that he's learned he can't run away from it, and so has come to welcome it into his life. Listen to the whole interview at bit.ly/patinkin.

Despite the countless times I'd told people they could always start over, it did not occur to me that I could rip out stitches and start again if I screwed the doll up. It did not occur to me that it was a party and not, like, open-heart surgery. It did not occur to me that people weren't paying any attention to what I was doing, and that my little project couldn't matter less to them.

It felt like hours passed (really minutes), and I just sat there, slumped over my drink.

But oh, I did so love that ugly fabric. I'd sneak sideways glances at it, and felt fiercely competitive about it—I was desperate that no one else would take it.

In the end, my love for the fabric beat out my fear of being found out, so I decided I would just make the doll ugly. I wouldn't fret about how you're supposed to sew a doll. I wouldn't care if my seams were uneven. I would just do it. I would do it with abandon. And I would try to make it as ugly as I possibly could, for real.

I cut two almost-matching doll-shaped pieces out of the fabric, sewed them together most of the way around, and stuffed the doll within an inch of its life. Then I applied a truly gruesome seam to close it up, held her (it was obviously a her) at an arm's length, and decided she needed to accessorize. So I crocheted her a hideous scarf, and it felt amazing to feel comfortable knowing how to do that. Finally, I found some awful glass buttons and hot-glued them to her face. I had fun. I felt free—uninhibited and unencumbered and unedited.

I named the doll Shoshana,* and I loved her. And when I held her up to show her off, and people made their faces blank like they didn't know how to politely react, I announced, "I made her ugly on purpose! Her name is Shoshana! I totally love her!"

I don't remember any conversations from that night. I'm not sure if we sang to Ian. There may have been cupcakes? But I do remember being utterly consumed by making that doll. I remember the lightness that replaced the tightness in my chest. I remember delighting in finding the ugliest buttons in the bowl.

I still have the doll.

I've since learned to sew.

---

* No reason; it's just the name that seemed appropriate at the time. It eventually became clear that I'm inclined to name all my ugly creatures. No name has significance; I just choose one that feels right. Also, it seems wrong to attribute a made-up backstory to a creature and not give it a name.

One evening a few years after Ian's party, I was coming home on the bus, staring out the window. To the rhythm of storefronts passing by, my mind wandered back to Shoshana. I'd spoken to colleagues and crafters about how freeing it had been to make something ugly on purpose, how unusual it was, how there's such pressure to create beauty, especially in the crafts world, and how that pressure can be defeating. But I hadn't given it any more thought than that. On the bus, though, as I daydreamed, I realized that every person in the world should make something ugly on purpose. Crafters, naturally, could use a break from the pressures of cute and desirable, even if it would make them uncomfortable. Artists could gain unexpected perspective. Engineers might see the way they solve problems a little differently after they'd made something that would typically be considered a failure. Entrepreneurs, for sure, could use taking a step back to stare down their fear of failing.

I ran home from the bus and told my partner I'd had an **IDEA**.

An hour later, I'd registered MightyUgly.com and had started populating the site with these notions:

THAT UGLY CAN BE WONDERFUL. THAT STRIVING FOR IT CAN BE LIBERATING. THAT STARING IT DOWN CAN TAKE ITS POWER AWAY, SO WE STOP PREVENTING OURSELVES FROM DOING BIG THINGS.

Ugly is failure. It's shame. It's doubt.

But ugly can make us mighty. All we have to do is pay attention to it. When we look at it, when we stare it right in the face, we take its power for our own. We grow to understand it. We learn from it. We defuse it.

And we become free.

SECTION 1: HEROES

ON FLIPPING THINGS AROUND

One summer day, I parked at the side of a wooded road to listen to an interview on CBC Radio. *Writers and Company* host Eleanor Wachtel had spoken with Joyce Carol Oates, and the prolific author talked about her belief that there are some people in life that we forget; and, well, we're just not meant to remember them. She likened this to Medusa—how we can safely look at her reflected in a mirror, but if we look at her directly, we're turned to stone.

Many of the experiences I write about in this book didn't become meaningful to me until long after they happened. Certainly when I was nine years old, I didn't have the perspective or the awareness to think about my experiences in any context but the immediate one. But even struggles and triumphs I've experienced in full color as an adult have taken on new clearer meaning for me upon reflection through the mirror of Mighty Ugly.

For example, I've discovered I have a habit, when stuck, of turning expected assumptions upside down.

When I was in college, I took a class on contemporary literature. I was (and remain) a relatively slow reader, and I was forced to accept early in the semester that I simply wasn't going to be able to finish reading all dozen or so novels according to the schedule of our syllabus—despite the nagging fact that for the first time in my life, all the required titles were novels I actually wanted to read.* The novel that affected me most profoundly was William Faulkner's *Light in August*, about, among other themes, an unwed pregnant woman in the deep South of the 1930s. I fell in love with Faulkner's language, so

---

* The only one I managed to finish was *Deliverance*. Make of that what you will.

in love that I lingered on every page and was barely able to complete half the novel before the due date of the five-page paper I had to write about it. In a frenzied panic the night before the deadline, I hung my head and picked up a copy of the CliffsNotes for the novel, just so I could be sure of how it all ended.

Much of our in-class discussion about the story revolved around the passivity of the protagonist. In a fit of pique, desperate for a clear idea to write my five pages about, I decided I'd focus on how, contrary to all our talk, Lena Grove was actually strong. Was this idea mentioned in the CliffsNotes? I can't remember.

I handed my paper to my graduate-student teaching assistant on time, in a cold sweat.

A couple of weeks later, he returned the papers, and when he handed me mine, he smiled. At the top, in sharp red pen, was "A" and a note that said something like, "Graduate material. If I could give you a higher mark, I would."

My reaction was mixed. Initially, I was elated—that was the highest praise I'd ever received on a paper. But by the time I reached the classroom door and turned to walk back to my dorm room, I felt an increasing sense of despair. If the paper I wrote as an early undergraduate, at the last possible moment, on a theme I came up with out of desperation, was graduate material, then what value could graduate study possibly hold? I couldn't look my TA in the eye again, despite his sudden treatment of me as a star pupil. *He* was a grad student, and what did that even mean anymore?

I've gone back and forth about this experience ad nauseum over the last twentyish years. On the one hand, the ideas in that paper were mine, and the writing was mine, so I suppose the praise was fair. On the other hand, it was a load of BS and I knew it.

Over time, I've come to recognize that toying with expectations is at the heart of my creative drive. When I struggle to make sense of something, I try to look at it from a completely different perspective.

When I hit a snag in a craft project, I put it aside for a while and when I go back to it, I try to do the opposite of what I originally wanted to achieve. When I'm blocked, I see if I can shift my focus entirely. When I'm paralyzed by the pressure to make something mind-blowingly awesome, I make something ugly instead.

I love making the simplest of tried-and-true crafts—garter-stitch shawls, granny square blankets, patchwork quilts—but when my hands itch to make something more unique, I find I especially enjoy taking the most established assumptions and just messing around with them. When I crochet dolls in a style usually associated with cuteness, for example, I make my dolls grotesque.

After my *Light in August* experience in college, I spent a lot of time identifying all the other ways that I felt like a fraud—all the other ways I faked it at the last minute, got away with cutting corners, and just generally didn't know as much as I thought I should—and I was terrified that someone would find out someday. Just as, when I was working in the yarn-crafts world, for a long time I kept it to myself that I rarely finished any project I started.

Watch Karen Walrond's TEDxHouston talk about how we see—really see—other people. Her perspective on what she calls "beautiful different" is breathtaking, as is her book, *The Beauty of Different*. Watch the video at bit.ly/beautifuldifferent.

Over time, though, I've come to very much value the tactic of flipping the expected on its head. Mighty Ugly is yet another thing I do in that manner. In a sea of *Rah! Rah! You can do it!*, I'm inclined to say, "Now hold on a minute—what does that *mean*? Why should I care that someone I barely know insists I can do it? Doesn't anyone care that at this particular moment, *I* don't actually think I can do it? Who has something to say about *that*?"

Well, to my occasional self and to you, I say this: *I get it.* It's OK that you're struggling, and it's OK that it hurts, and it's OK that you feel defeated or like a fraud sometimes. I get that it can be scary to break out of the belief that you're not creative or talented or skilled or gifted or ordained with some divine facility for making the perfect cupcake icing. It's true that sometimes we all fail miserably. It's just not OK to use that as an excuse not to try. For the rest of this book, we're going to try very hard to work through all that, so it'll get easier to try things anyway, to believe that you should, and to believe that you can.

Get ready.

FROM LOST TO FOUND

For most of my life, I insisted I was not creative. I didn't enjoy art class in school. I did not make stuff. I felt that I was an odd person; I did not fit in. I was awed by creative people, though. Silent and intimidated, I liked being around them, but I felt unworthy of their full attention because I knew I had nothing to give them back.

Eventually, I cured myself of this mistaken belief, but long before I discovered—or maybe just accepted—that creativity plays a central role in my life, I did something on a whim that changed everything. It set me on a very bumpy course through my insecurities, shame, and doubts, and spit me out on the other side equipped with a bit of purpose and a healthy dose of contentment. And more than one hobby.

The thing I did on a whim was this: I got really pissed off about crochet.*

It was a gloomy weekend afternoon in late February 2004, and I'd just spent hours combing the internet for crochet patterns. Many hours. Allow me to set the stage.

----

* Oh, were you expecting something different?

Knit blogging and online magazines were finding some serious traction in 2004. I'd learned how to knit the previous year and enjoyed all the online resources; I'd just progressed to learning how to crochet, and I assumed I'd find the same online landscape for the sister craft. What I discovered that afternoon was that I was wrong. Very, very wrong.

Blurry photos of doilies and purple websites with blinking text were all I found. No proper crochet blogs. No online crochet magazines. I didn't understand why, but I couldn't accept the reality of it, and I didn't know enough about crochet yet to do anything about it.

So I assumed I was doing the internet wrong, and I put my head down and searched some more, and found more of nothing. Until I realized that part of why I was so annoyed was that the websites I kept finding were just so awful, with the blinking and the blurry. I may not have known enough about crochet to share any knowledge on that front, but I did know how to make a website that didn't have blinking text. I did know how to take a photo that wasn't blurry. I did know how to say what I meant. And so that's what I did—on a lark, I made a website, and I decided to call it Crochet Me.*

When I launched the site, it consisted of a hastily cobbled-together logo, and blank pages for patterns and articles that I planned to fill with contributions from people who had fabulous crochet to share. On the home page, I wrote a sort of manifesto.** I decried the state of crochet online, admitted to my status as a crochet ignoramus, suggested

----

* I have a voice in my head that, come to think of it, sounds a lot like my dad's voice; it replies immediately to any statement in the form of "___ you" with, "No, ___ YOU." Like, "Hey, you." "No, hey YOU." Anyway. Crochet Me. No, Crochet YOU.'

** About crochet! I know. Look, we all have things that rile us up in ways that other people don't understand. I *still* get my knickers in a twist about crochet. Doesn't mean I don't also get nuts about political injustices and climate change, OK? OK.

I might not be the only person who felt this way, and volunteered my knowledge of building websites* to create one about crochet that was **GOOD** and **NOT-BLINKING**.

I linked to my new site on a couple of forums and then I think I went to bed.

Ten days after I launched the manifesto, I was hearing from people from all over the world. Up to that point, I had used the web as a playground for learning HTML code and looking stuff up. Suddenly, I was using the web to interact with people for whom English was a third language. And those people thought my idea was awesome, and they wanted to be a part of it.

For real?

For real.

> There's an actual thing called *impostor syndrome* that leads people to dismiss their successes as being due to luck or fakery. Lauren Bacon, an author and business coach (read more about her on page 66), has written extensively about this. One of her blog posts, in particular, is a great place to start reading about this belief so many of us have that someday we'll be found out as frauds: bit.ly/impostor-syndrome.

In our current world of viral videos and people getting sick of Facebook, this might not seem like a big deal, so allow me to remind you that this all was happening a year before YouTube even launched, when the social web was still a wee seed, not even sprouting. And I was e-mailing with a woman from France about writing crochet articles.

----

* Hand-coding HTML! Table-based layouts! Why to always save photographs as a JPG, not a GIF!

I spent the next two and a half years chasing this thing I started while it ran at top speed, taunting me to keep up.

At the time I started Crochet Me, I was unhappily trying to hack it as a freelance web designer who was great with the code but not so much the design. I'd bitten off more than I could chew with one of my clients, and not in a good way. And then suddenly I had this crochet thing on the side that was taking up more and more of my time, as more and more people submitted patterns and articles, and more and more people used those patterns and read those articles. For Crochet Me, I was sitting high on the confidence side of the seesaw inside my mind, keeping an eye on the insecure side but keeping it down on the ground. For the first time in my life, I knew I was onto something, and it felt terrific. So I decided that rather than berating myself for failing at the web-design business I'd set out to build, I ditched it without looking back (after completing that daunting contract the best I could) so I could pursue the project that was actually making me happy.

One day a couple of years after I launched Crochet Me, I discovered I'd become a magazine editor. With the help of a couple of volunteers and dozens of contributors, we were publishing issues on a regular basis to a rapidly growing audience. Design submissions came in at a good clip, and I'd jumped the daunting hurdle of having to reject some. I worked with designers to flesh out their ideas. I worked with volunteer technical editors who took on the responsibility of making sure the patterns were accurate and clearly written. I requested that blurry photos be retaken. I blogged regularly and fielded reader questions. I wrote a column about cool crochet in a print knitting magazine. I attended conferences and trade shows, and one day it dawned on me that I had built a proper career for myself. (I still looked at my feet and mumbled that I ran a crochet website when people asked what I did for work. I still shuffled around when I spoke with *Industry Professionals*, because I was an internet freak who worked in my basement and they worked in an office for a salary.)

At a trade show, I had made the acquaintance of a print magazine publisher. One day, this publisher e-mailed asking to set up a phone call. On the call, she explained that she was looking for a new editor for the annual crochet issue they published (spun off from their knitting magazine). She wanted to know if I could think of anyone who was qualified and might be interested. My mind drew a blank, and I told her I'd be in touch if anyone came to mind.

When I hung up the phone, I was struck by a terrifying thought. Was she feeling *me* out? No, she couldn't be. I was a hack! An internet fake-it-till-you-make-it neophyte. I had no formal experience in publishing. No training. No degree. No. She was asking out of genuine interest in my opinion, only. I knew people she didn't know.

But then.

I couldn't actually think of anyone. None of the people I knew had any interest in being a magazine editor. It's part of why Crochet Me had ended up so visible—not many people had started up *other* crochet magazines online. I couldn't think of anyone who might be interested in a magazine editing job.

I talked to my husband, Greg. "Do you think she was feeling me out?" Of course he had no way to know. "What should I do?"

He asked if I'd be interested. Funny that. What an obvious question I hadn't even asked myself.

"Oh. Um. Hells yes," I said.

So I had to figure out how to make up for the fact that I either hadn't clued in to the real reason for her call while we were still on the phone together, or to suggest myself in a way that would lead her to see me as a viable candidate if she didn't already see me that way.

I sent her an e-mail. I can't remember exactly what I wrote, but I believe it went something like, "Hi. I'm not sure if you've considered me as a possible candidate for the job, but I'd like to throw my hat into the ring." I'm sure it was more long-winded than that, full of qualifications that made me feel comfortable being so bold, so presumptuous.

And then, more phone conversations ensued. She flew me to Colorado to see the offices and meet the people. Nothing formal was ever stated—I wasn't told I was a candidate; I wasn't told I was formally interviewing. I was a mess of nerves **CONSTANTLY**.

I spent a day and a half in Colorado for the "is-it-an-interview?" I crashed and burned the first day. I was timid and ingratiating, so bowled over by being there that I felt and behaved more like a doe-eyed fangirl than a prospective hire. I called Greg that night from the sidewalk outside the Hampton Inn. Pacing manically, I freaked out. I utterly melted down.

> **"Instead of inhibiting me, I think that slight fear propels me forward. Because the alternative? The alternative is allowing that fear to consume me. So forward, really, is the only option."**
>
> —BETSY CROSS, JEWELRY DESIGNER

And then I taught myself a lesson I've worked hard not to forget. All was not lost. I had the next day. I needed to put my game face on, and I needed to show up, and I needed to do the work.

I'd never felt such resolve. I slept like a baby, and I did put my game face on the next morning. Like they do in the movies, I stared long and hard at myself in the bathroom mirror. Starting at my early breakfast meeting, I behaved like an adult—a smart and capable one. I shared my opinions and I listened. Three months later, I started my new job.

It was the first time in five years I had a boss, and I loved it. At first. Being hired reminded me that the work I did with Crochet Me was, as I'd suspected but not allowed myself to believe, valid. The skills I'd developed were worth something. I felt recognized and capable.

In his classic 1972 book *The Inner Game of Tennis: The Classic Guide to the Mental Side of Peak Performance*, Timothy Gallwey explores what many athletes call "being in the zone" and what the rest of us call "flow"—the phase in which your mental state and physical actions are so harmoniously in sync that you're completely absorbed. The mental gymnastics I did after I beat myself up for performing so terribly in my interview were the closest I had ever come to deliberately getting into the flow. Of all the weird things I could have thought of, I actually tried to imagine what a football player might think to himself before stepping onto the field to endure a world of physical pain. (I can't stand football.) I thought of the resolve. The confidence. The purpose that made the pain seem worth it. Before going to bed that night, I envisioned myself with black paint under my eyes. I had one chance, and I had to make the most of it. I still do this when I'm teetering on the edge of self-doubt. "Get it together, Werker. You need to get this done. You can cry about it later." (And I sometimes do.)

If you want to experience being in the flow more frequently, or otherwise take a gander at how your mind and body interact in your craft, art, or athletic activities, *The Inner Game of Tennis* is a classic for good reason.

My first six months at *Interweave Crochet* were a wild ride, and provided me a lesson I'll do well to remember: I love me a steep learning curve. Print! It works so differently than digital! New lingo, new workflows, new budget. I was on fire. I got to do the work I loved best—collaborating with designers to publish amazing crochet—in an industry that, until then, I'd only been on the periphery of. It was, and still is, an exciting time in publishing, as the status quo that endured for decades upon decades continues to be dramatically shaken up. Another lesson I learned: I do so love a good shake-up.

HERO QUALITIES

SELF-DOUBT

We're going to get right to the heart of it, friends. There's one thing we need to count on moving forward. Without it, Mighty Ugly and the other exercises on these pages are nothing but benign activities. With it, the essays and insights and exercises could possibly transform your daily life. Not to get melodramatic about it, but for real.

The beating heart of Mighty Ugly—the weapon that will enable and empower you to do the work and battle your creative demons—is **HONESTY**.

And it's the hardest kind of honesty around: honesty with yourself. Someone else being honest with you, even if their words hurt—we can shield ourselves against that pain in some ways. Unfiltered, unfettered honesty with ourselves, though? There's no salve to protect us from the pain of that. But there's also nothing to protect us from the good of it. The promise I make to you right now is that there is absolutely, without a doubt, joy in being honest with yourself. Eventually.

Our focus on examining, combatting, and embracing the ugly parts of what we're going to uncover should not take away from the fact that alongside your demons are already heroes. HEROES, I tell you.

So before we get to the painful part, we're going to start with the part that might be difficult, but shouldn't hurt too badly.

On the following pages, write down your strengths. Start with THINGS I'M GOOD AT. Write things down! Big or small. Make an organized list, or just jot things down willy-nilly. Whatever you want. Even if they're things you're inclined to discount as irrelevant or inconsequential—write them down. What are you proud to have achieved, even if it was a long time ago? When have you surprised yourself by doing something awesome? What do your friends rely on you for? What makes your kid smile? What do you do effortlessly that you've seen others struggle with? If you're ace at flossing your teeth, write it down. If you once delivered a baby on a stuck elevator, write it down. Have a knack for folding the laundry? Great at writing book reports? Master of the internet search?

When you're done, take a step back. Look at your list and try to come up with common themes that tie some of the traits together. Use different colored highlighters or crayons to help; mark like things with the same color. For example, if you delivered a baby on a stuck elevator, and also once made friends with a stranger when you were stranded in an airport overnight, mark those as "optimistic in a crisis" or "cool-headed when things go sideways." As you start to see patterns, take some notes so you can examine those relationships more closely.

You may need to be creative to connect the dots, or the connections may seem totally obvious. If many of your strengths involve making things, even different sorts of things like food and promises, that could be a theme. If several strengths are about people, try to figure out what's at the heart of that—is it being empathetic, or funny, or valuing family and friends? Maybe a few items are about intellectual pursuits—do you read a lot? Are you an expert on a particular topic? Are you generally curious? A skeptic? Could be you're a great crafter, a nurturing friend, a talented musician, a natural leader. Or all of the above. Don't feel you need to rely on conventional labels here; take poetic license in your interpretation of your strengths.

Your strengths are qualities that make you feel good and maybe even make others feel good. They may involve having a talent for something you feel innately good at, or they may be related to achievements you've worked very hard for. They may involve personality traits or a special way of approaching a certain kind of situation. Maybe you're a free spirit who can always be counted on for a last-minute road trip, or maybe you're a full-on Type A who always makes sure an adventure is fully planned well in advance. Either way, it's a strength.

Allow yourself to see a hero even in the small things. If you can whip up a delicious dinner for four with thirty minutes' notice, that's a heck of a hero quality. As much, I'd argue, as knowing how to siphon gas in a dire situation on the side of a dusty rural road, and doing it without complaint. (I'd complain.)

Sit with your list for a while. This shouldn't be something you give only a brief thought to; it should be something you allow to percolate in your mind for some time. It's very easy to enumerate our own flaws, and we spend an awful lot of time allowing thoughts of those flaws to infiltrate our day-to-day. This exercise is about focusing on the opposite for a change, and you should work on it until you're smiling.

This exercise can be daunting, I know. Here's an example of how it might be completed, to give you an idea. Take Shoshana, the ugly doll, and let's pretend she's a person. Shoshana is the executive assistant to a sexist pig who is the CEO of a company she really believes in. She lives in a modest apartment with her dog, Astro, her best friend is her sister, Rose, and she's active in her synagogue's women's group. In her spare time, she reads romance novels, and though she'd really like to take up cross-stitch, she doesn't know where to start and is embarrassed to ask.

On the **THINGS I'M GOOD AT** page, Shoshana listed the following:

* Very tidy
* Good with dogs
* OK phone voice
* Very organized
* Good at motivating others
* Punctual
* Can recite key *Pride and Prejudice* dialogue from memory

She pulled out her colored pencils and circled "very tidy," "very organized," and "punctual" in red. Then she circled "good with dogs" and "good at motivating others" in blue. After thinking about it for a while, she decided that at the heart of the red items is that she values order, and is good at maintaining it. At the heart of the blue items, she figures, is that she can lead from a place of authority and mutual respect. Given the other items on the list, she decides there are a few more things at the heart of her strengths: she's loyal and reliable, and when she's passionate about something, she becomes an expert in that thing. Also, given what a pig her boss is and how she manages to keep him in line, she realizes she's able to hold her own in unpleasant conditions if she's able to do meaningful work; in other words, she's strong and persistent. (And she secretly fantasizes about him getting fired.)

Now. On the THE HEART OF WHAT I'M GOOD AT page, write down these overarching themes you've discovered, and write them big. These characteristics help to define who you are, and I want you to remember them as we proceed through the difficult slog of identifying the demons that are quite opposite from these heroes. I want you to remember them both because you should give yourself credit where it's due, and because these characteristics will be the most effective weapons you'll have in your arsenal as we begin to wage The Great Demon War. I won't be able to walk you through how to use these weapons, since every person's arsenal will be different—I'm relying on you to trust yourself. Trust that these qualities you have are the real deal. Trust that you aren't bragging when you accept them about yourself. You owe it to yourself to accept the goodness in you, and you owe it to yourself to use that goodness to fight your demons.

THINGS I AM GOOD AT

THE HEART OF WHAT I'M GOOD AT

It's possible that you stared at those blank pages and couldn't write anything down. It happens. I want you to call someone awesome and have a chat. Come back to this when you're ready, but don't proceed to name your demons till you've first named your heroes.

Do feel free to revisit your hero pages at any time. You may see them differently at different times or in different moods; add or subtract some over time, but deny any inclination you may feel in your darkest hours to erase them all. Even when you're feeling your worst, your hero qualities persist. I swear.

OK, this is the end of my pep talk. I recognize that this may have been hard for you, or it may have been a piece of cake—either way, your having done it means we're ready to proceed.

SECTION 2: VILLAINS

ON VULNERABILITY

The following exercises are intended to be difficult. If you breeze right through, convinced you're free of demons and have no work to do, I'll say right here before we even get started that you're full of it. Don't do that. Don't let yourself off easy. If you feel embarrassed, feel it. If you feel ashamed or angry or frustrated or defeated or sad, feel it. It's OK to feel it. You can only help yourself to stop feeling it if you get to know that pain first. When you're squirming, come back to the Hero Qualities exercise you just did. Rip those pages out and stick them to the wall. Allow it to remind you that you are not defined by your demons. Allow yourself to believe in all the good. These are the heroes that will swoop in and save the day, as heroes do.

Brené Brown is a researcher who studies vulnerability. "Vulnerability sounds like truth and feels like courage," she says on her website. "Truth and courage aren't always comfortable, but they're never weakness." In her powerful TEDxHouston talk on this subject (which is required viewing), she points out that shame—the feeling that we're not good enough, the fear of disconnection from other people—gets worse the less we talk about it, and that vulnerability is at the heart of living fully. Spend some time at bit.ly/brene-brown.

On Fear and Taking a Compliment

It's one thing to sit down and make something. It's another thing entirely for someone else to see what you've made. Certainly, there's much joy and satisfaction to be found in making things just for yourself and never letting them out into the greater world. But don't let anxiety about what other people think be the driving force behind your desire to keep your creations to yourself.

When Stacy Rozich was a teenager and wanted to be a professional artist, she struggled mightily with fear of rejection. "I knew I had at least a foundation of raw talent, but it was still embarrassing for anyone to take a peek at what my imagination would come up with. My mother would have friends over and call me over to show my drawings to them, and it would mortify me. I also didn't know what to do with myself when I was complimented: do a little dance? Wave my hands around?

"My father is a commercial artist; his journey is inspiring, but still a cautionary tale. By the time he was married and had two kids, he worked any job he could to pay the bills and put food on the table, while working as a sign painter or commercial menu board artist on the weekends. His dedication and quality of work eventually led to him working at his craft full time, but not until he was in his fifties. When I told my mother I wanted to go to art school, she practically face-palmed and said, 'Really? You really want to go through that?' I did."

Now, Stacey is a successful gallery artist and has steady work doing commissions and illustration. Still, she struggles with how to interpret her clients' responses to her art. "I am such an enthusiastic person if I enjoy something, and it's taken me a while to realize not a lot of people wear their happiness on their sleeve like I do. When I don't get the appropriate amount of excitement that, say, *I* would show, I think, 'Do they not like it? Where's my parade?' It just shows how lucky I am with the success of past projects that I take subtle happiness as not being happy at all."

"Never confuse a single defeat with a final defeat."

As a teenager, Jia Jiang had big entrepreneurial dreams. When he was about to turn thirty, he realized he'd settled into a comfortable life, but was no longer pursuing those dreams. Four days before his first child was born, he quit his job at the urging of his wife. She told him to take six months to pursue those dreams; he could always go get a new job if nothing panned out.

Midway through this adventure, Jiang experienced a major rejection that left him wanting to just give up. But then he started thinking about his experience of rejection, and how fear of further rejection was keeping him from continuing to try. So he set out to build up his resistance to the power of rejection by seeking it out, doing things he was sure would lead to rejection so he could thicken his skin. He asked a cop if he could drive his car. He asked a pilot if he could fly his plane. He knocked on a stranger's door and asked if he could play soccer in the backyard. And what he discovered was that, more often than not, people actually said yes.

"Rejection is constant," Jiang said in a talk at the 2013 World Domination Summit. And it is. When we allow the inevitability of rejection to hold us back from trying in the first place, we also prevent the *yeses* from happening.

Rejection is different from failure. Failure is the end—sure, it can also be the beginning, but failure indicates an exhaustion of possibilities. Rejection is one setback. It's one person saying no. There's always another person to ask and another way to do the asking.

Watch Jiang's whole talk at bit.ly/jiajiang.

THE UGLY VOICE

There's a voice in the back of your mind. Do you hear it?

It tells you you suck. It tells you you're not good enough and never have been. It tells you you're undeserving. You're not doing it right. You've never done it right. You'll never do it right. Don't bother. **WHO DO YOU THINK YOU ARE?**

You do hear it, right?

Some people refer to this voice as *negative self-talk.* That makes sense, since anything going on in your own mind is a part of yourself. I don't find it terribly *useful* to think of this voice as self-talk, though, no matter how accurate the moniker, because to confront that voice would mean to confront myself, which would essentially mean I'd be beating myself up from both sides. I can see no good reason to do that, so I don't, but that solves nothing and the voice just goes on and on and on.

So I think of my voice as belonging to a very wee green man. He's naked and has knobbly knees and elbows, and tremendous ears. He's like halfway between Gollum and a Smurf, with a little bit of Dobby, the *Harry Potter* house-elf, thrown in for good measure. But, seriously: entirely green, including his bald head.

He rarely yells at me, but his quiet voice is even worse, like how you know a parent is really mad when they get still and calm instead of screaming their head off.

The little green man tells me my work is terrible and that no one will like it. He tells me I'm unqualified and delusional to strive for my goals. He tells me I'm undeserving of praise. He throws his hands in the air and wonders aloud who the hell I think I am.

He is my constant companion, and he whispers his piercing words to me without relent. I've tried to ignore him, but it's exhausting. I inevitably let my guard down, and in seeps his slithering degradation.

A couple of acting students once told me they had an instructor who called the ugly voice a *fear gremlin*. I've since learned the term isn't unique to this particular instructor (Google it). To learn how to stop the gremlin from crippling their confidence and blocking their creative expression, the students had to get to know it, then make some kind of physical representation of it, and then confront it—in class, in front of everyone. This is why I find it so much more useful to personify my ugly voice as a little green man rather than think of it as part of myself: I can confront the little green man far more easily than I can confront myself, which means I actually end up feeling better. And after the confrontation is over, when my wounds have healed a little, I can go back and examine how the green man was really me.

That said, I didn't personify my ugly voice as the little green man until I actually noticed it was in my head. It can be very easy not to notice something that's always there. Once I discovered the voice, and spent some time teasing its words from my deliberate internal monologue, it quickly came to inhabit the verdant Gollum-Smurf body I now see so clearly in my mind. I could certainly see the value in the acting students' exercise. When fighting an enemy, best make it an enemy you can see.

> **"I identified my inner critic recently as being that shouty, cross Scottish voice at the end of Pink Floyd's 'Another Brick In The Wall': 'If you don't eat your meat, you can't have any pudding! How can you have any pudding if you don't eat your meat?!'"**
>
> —KIRSTY HALL, ARTIST

FEAR OF FAILURE   SELF-DOUBT   PERFECTIONISM

I'm about to ask you to do something that will hurt, and I want you to know I know it will hurt. It won't be fun, and I won't be there to hand you a lollipop or a tissue or a stiff drink when you're done. I'm telling you this because before I ask you to do this thing, I'm going to ask you to prepare to take care of yourself.

Prepare to take care of yourself. Wait to do this exercise until you're feeling pretty good—don't do it right after you've encountered an ego-crushing defeat. Gather some items or people that will help you out if you need it when you're done—a box of tissues, a hip flask, a night out dancing.

Here goes.

Close your eyes, and listen to your ugly voice. If you've never noticed it in there, embark upon a quest inside your mind to find it. Telltale signs to look for: cobwebby corners you instinctually avoid, a feeling of anxiety as you approach, fear, sweat. If you've tuned out your ugly voice intentionally or unintentionally, you may need to put in a little effort to let your guard down. If, at the other extreme, it's shouting too loudly to hear it clearly, take a deep breath and work to modulate it so you can understand what it's saying.

ON THE NEXT PAGES, WRITE DOWN WHAT THE VOICE SAYS. It may say one thing over and over and over in an endless maddening mantra, or it might deliver a laundry list of ugliness.

Write it down.

All of it. Don't shy away.

Step away if you need a break. Unplug the phone if you need to. Pour yourself some liquid courage.

Keep in mind that writing it down doesn't make it right or true. It just makes it so you can know your demons well enough to deal them some serious damage.

WHAT THE UGLY VOICE SAYS

When I first started listening to my ugly voice, I thought that what I was hearing were my deepest, darkest truths. It told me I'm a flake who can't or won't follow through on my promises or big ideas. It told me I was a freak, since I struggled to cope with circumstances everyone else seemed to take in stride. It told me I thought far too highly of myself, given my lack of credentials or recognizable achievement. It called me a freak, again, for not wanting "normal" things, and for wanting "abnormal" things.

This is the power of the ugly voice: we think it's telling us the truth, and we believe it.

But it's not telling us the truth. Or, at least it's not telling us the whole truth. In part that's because it's a slick manipulator and a liar, and in part that's because we are able to change.

Nobody is perfect, and that means each of us has qualities that aren't so hot. So, naturally, some of what the ugly voice tells us is true. That's why we tremble in its presence and try so hard to avoid it to begin with. What the voice omits from its monologue is that all of us are flawed, so any one person's being flawed does not actually set them apart.

So yes, some of what the voice tells us rings true. Without that element of truth, its words wouldn't hurt. What the voice chooses not to ask you is what you're going to do about it. You can do anything you want. You can wallow in your belief that the voice is right, and you really do suck for all the reasons it outlines in so much vivid detail, or you can combat the truth, point by point.

Perfection isn't the goal; that would be crazy. The goal is to take the ugly voice's power away so it stops holding us back. This is what Mighty Ugly is about. We personify our ugly voice by naming the demons it creates in our minds, then we slay them (and slay them again), and then we get on with life.

The Truth of the Ugly Voice

Betsy Cross is the designer behind the jewelry line Betsy & Iya. I didn't know her when I first bought myself a pair of her earrings and a necklace, but I did know that I was utterly in love with her style. I eventually met her in person, and I knew when I started writing this book that if I asked her about her creative demons, she'd give it to me straight. "[My ugly voice] is a little b. She has told me that I'm a fraud, that I don't have enough style to do what I'm doing. Every single time I'm about to release a new collection, she tells me that it's no cooler than an infant's stack of Legos, or that my sketches were done by baby hands, or that I'm just straight-up fooling people. She even tells me my hair looks ridiculous or that my eyes are uneven. She tells me that every single other designer's work that exists in the world far exceeds mine and there is no possible way I could catch up."

Ouch.

And still, season after season, Betsy releases new lines that are like nothing I've seen before and yet totally embody her style. I derive great comfort knowing that she battles the same doubt and insecurity and fear that I do, and yet there she is, killing it.

"Somewhere in that dirty, dark wormhole of my own self telling me I'm not good enough," she wrote to me, "I realize that I am guilty of *most* of her accusations. What's cool, though, is when I recognize that I wouldn't be me if my hair didn't look ridiculous or my sketches weren't wild and free, the way a child might sketch. And my work wouldn't be what it is if I were a perfect designer or if I tried to be cool or pretend that I'm a fashionista. So really, I turn it around and beat her at her own game. She points things out and tries to put them in a corner and paint them in a negative light—it's up to me to show her where they really want to stand."

Exactly.

Creative demons, as I call them, are the little monsters our ugly voice creates to do its bidding. They're the insidious gnats that gang up on us to make us miserable and stop us from making and doing the things we want.

The way I see it, there are three kinds of demons that spawn two other kinds of demons. This is not science, and it may not be in line with how you already, or will eventually grow to, think of your creative demons. But for the sake of mounting a solid offensive, Mighty Ugly–style, let's consider:

MAJOR DEMONS

FEAR OF FAILURE   SELF-DOUBT   PERFECTIONISM

MINOR DEMONS

PROCRASTINATION   BLOCK

The minor demons are symptoms of the presence of one or more of the major demons. When we're under attack, we feel blocked and/or we procrastinate.

Let's examine further.

MAJOR DEMONS

Fear of Failure

Have you ever sat across a desk from someone who tented their fingers, leaned back in their chair, and asked how risk-averse you are?

Risk aversion has to do with how comfortable you are taking risks. One's level of risk aversion varies with the type of decision being considered. Some people are averse to taking financial risks, but go sky-diving every weekend. Some people will only drive cars with the highest safety ratings, but don't bat an eye when their kid licks the bus window.

In the context of creative expression, risk is a little harder to talk about sometimes because the consequences of a decision can be very hard to predict. It's easy to say, "If I invest in this risky stock and the stock plummets, I'll lose my money; if it soars, I'll be rich." But what does one say when it comes to picking up a paintbrush for the first time? "If I put this brush to canvas and create something . . ." I couldn't even finish this sentence. ". . . pretty? But wait, whose definition of pretty? I could think it's pretty, but someone else might think it's awful." Get my drift?

It's almost perversely easy to fall down a rabbit hole of fear, because creative expression is so personal. We're talking about our ideas here, our vision. Our execution. We are entirely responsible for it. If we show someone and they don't like it, what does that mean for us? And if we, ourselves, don't like it? How sad and frustrating that would be.

There's a greater context that we often overlook when we're consumed by our own perceived defeat, though. And that's the context of how we so often conflate *failure* with *mistake*.

Failure is the end of the road; mistakes are all the times we screw up before we get there. Mistakes are far easier to handle when we keep in mind that we can always try again. This is what always surprises me when new crocheters or knitters tell me they're paralyzed by fear of screwing up—no yarn is harmed if you rip it back and start again. And it's what I try to keep in mind when I (almost always) feel intimidated by a sewing project—my seam ripper is my friend.

If we decide to view every mistake we make—and my goodness, we make so many mistakes—as a failure, well, that would be crippling, indeed.

My approach to combatting the Fear of Failure demon is to force myself to see my failure as a mistake.

Let's do a bit of a mental exercise to look more closely at how this works.

TRY THIS!

MISTAKES ALONG THE WAY

FEAR OF FAILURE

On the following page, list a few of your creative failures in the left-hand column. These could be projects that came out ugly, submissions that were rejected, gifts that went unappreciated, anything that gives you a pang of shame to look back upon, and that your ugly voice uses as a reason to convince you not to try that thing again.

Then, think about whether there's something you'd do differently if you were to try that thing again. A different color combination, learning a new skill to help it go more smoothly, using a different set of techniques or materials. Write this down in the right-hand column.

When you're done, you should have a list of failures alongside a list of approaches that might not lead to failure if you were to try again.

Ask yourself if it would be worthwhile to give it another go. Would it?

FLIP IT AROUND: Look back at successful projects you've made. What could you have done differently to make them fail? Or look at your list of failures and think about how you could have failed even more spectacularly.

A FAILURE   # A POSSIBLE REMEDY

Self-Doubt

This one is a doozy, because we do it entirely to ourselves with no help from others.

When I was twenty-four and sat down at a sewing machine for the first time since eighth grade home ec class, I quickly discovered I couldn't sew in a straight line. The result of this discovery is that my husband assembled the chuppah* we got married under, entirely by himself. For ten years after this, I believed I couldn't sew.

Obviously—this *is* painfully obvious, right?—I was perceiving my mistake as a failure. I eventually took my friend Jenny Ryan's** advice and practiced sewing lines through paper until I was comfortable doing it straight.

But it's self-doubt I'm focusing on here. For those ten years, I honestly believed I couldn't do it, and I honestly believed it wasn't worth trying. So I didn't sew. And in fact, a part of my crafty identity was that I didn't—couldn't—sew.

In more, shall we say, *significant* contexts, self-doubt has kept me from applying for contracts, from showing my work, from even mentioning that I'm interested in learning how to make a particular kind of thing. My doubt about myself renders me meek, and I don't like it.

Self-doubt is what makes me a crafty self-saboteur—as I get more and more nervous about my ability to follow through with an ambitious crafty project, I deliberately screw it up. I relieve my anxiety about not being skilled enough by displaying a lack of skill. Brilliant.

----

* A *chuppah* is a wedding canopy. We made ours long before I got to know my crafty self and developed any sort of personal style, so I actually find it pretty unattractive now. That said, it's obviously the most special quilt in our home. Eighteen people made squares for it, and poor Greg sat for hours at the machine putting it all together, bored out of his mind, a copy of *Quilting for Dummies* at his elbow.

** Her book *Sew Darn Cute: 30 Sweet & Simple Projects to Sew & Embellish* (St. Martin's Griffin, 2009) is, indeed, adorable.

The opposite of self-doubt isn't arrogance; it's confidence. And the only way I've found to combat doubt is to take tiny steps that prove to me my doubt is unfounded. One doesn't take a giant leap out of self-doubt; one just starts climbing the stairs.

Perfectionism

I once worked on a major project with a perfectionist. We had split the work up so we each had defined roles, and my major role was to flesh out her ideas and make sure they were written out clearly. Except she wouldn't give me her notes. And she wouldn't give me her first drafts. And eventually, I had to pry her not-quite-finished final copies from her clenched fists.

She was a perfectionist, and she just couldn't bear the thought of handing off something that wasn't polished to a healthy sheen.

Sound familiar?

I admit that I'm not a perfectionist, but many, many people who do my Mighty Ugly workshops are. They tell me how very hard it is for them not to work single-mindedly toward a perfect outcome, and how this need for flawlessness keeps them from even starting their projects sometimes. They tell me how hard it is to avoid symmetry, how terrifying it feels to show their work before they're certain it's done, how rules of color harmony are nearly impossible to ignore.

Perfection is a pipe dream, though, and when we loosen our grip on it even just a little bit, we finally allow ourselves to enjoy the process of making.

Variations

There are other major demons whose identities are not quite as crisply defined. Like **FEAR OF THE BLANK PAGE OR CANVAS**—the wide openness is so daunting, we freeze. This one is closely related to all of the other major demons—fear of failure (what if I start off wrong and just can't get it right after that?), self-doubt (what if I'm not actually capable of doing this?), perfectionism (what if at the very end of this project I haven't even started yet I can't get it exactly perfect)?

When I'm faced with a blank page and the paralyzing goal of creating a masterpiece, there are only two things I can do to get past the wall of block: I remind myself that I can't set out to create a masterpiece, and I just start writing. Same goes for crafting. (And for cleaning my house, which somehow always feels the same.)

I can't set out to create a masterpiece, because that would mean I'm totally full of myself. Also, I've learned most masterpieces aren't intentional; they're just regular projects that resonate unusually. All I can do is set out to make *something*, then try to make that something as good as it can be. In writing, that means I write fast and furiously, then revise ruthlessly. In revision, I can take out all the crap, and rewrite without the daunting challenge of having to fill a blank page.

In crafting, when I'm following instructions, I read through them once so I can grok the project, then I force myself to only pay attention to the very first step. Then I follow the next step only when I'm done with the first, and so on. Eventually, I'll find myself working away at a good clip, and only then will I allow myself to think about the bigger picture, about how all the time I'm spending on each step will combine into a whole that I want to love.

When I'm making it up as I go along, I approach making stuff like writing—my first go is always a draft. If it's terrible, I ditch it and start over. If it's mediocre, I ditch it but keep the good parts. If it's perfect, I wonder what kind of flaw will make itself known after I declare myself a genius.

In any medium, I also start out assuming—even planning—that I'll delete the first thing I do, whether it's a paragraph or the first few rows of a scarf. That makes those first steps far less precious and therefore less intimidating.

Now, other demons.

FEAR OF SUCCESS is a good one—what if I nail it? What do I do then? Failure stings, but there's certainty on the other side of it— don't do that same thing again. Success means you have to keep succeeding. It means people start counting on you. It means you have farther to fall.

> 99U.com is a resource for creative professionals, but you don't need to be a professional to benefit from it. For tips on combating fear of success, check out bit.ly/fear-of-success.

Then there's **PRESSURE FOR THE NEXT PIECE**, which comes after you make something great. What if the next thing you make isn't stunning and wonderful? What if it's just normal? What if you're not inspired to even make a next piece?

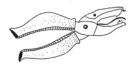

All of these demons can be tied, loosely or snugly, to one or more of the three major demons.

The thing to keep in mind is that there are no rules for how we experience our demons, and it's quite possible you're only truly plagued by one or two. As you proceed, try not to convince yourself you should be bothered by things you're not bothered by. Count those as gifts, and focus on the demons you really need to slay.

MINOR DEMONS

Procrastination

I procrastinate when I've committed to doing something I don't actually want to do, when I'm concerned I'll fail or be criticized harshly, or when I'm not sure I can do the task expertly. I also procrastinate when I'm not yet smelling the fear of running out of time—I waste time just so I can get to the point when a fire is lit under my ass, and I have no choice but to bear down and get it done.

Rather than browbeat myself for procrastinating, I've come to embrace it. Naturally, I like to try to figure out which demon is causing me to waste time. Usually it's fear of failure—I put off working on a project to put off failing at it. What I've come to accept is that my fear is OK, and sometimes I need to sit with it for a while and not make stuff. The better I get to know the fear, the less power it holds over me, and eventually I come to a place of telling myself I'm just going to make the thing anyway. Procrastination is my space for sorting out my fear.

Since procrastination is a regular part of my creative process, I do what I think of as *productive procrastination* (artist and author Noah Scalin [read more about him on the following page and on page 132] calls himself a *creative procrastinator*). Instead of wasting time looking at photos of sloths and owls and puppies, I do something that will make me feel accomplished. I'll work on another project, do a load of laundry, walk the dog, read a book, e-mail a friend. When I'm really torturing myself battling demons, I'll do my taxes or fill out some other kind of government form.

To become a productive procrastinator, I had to erase some of the lines I had drawn around my time. If I have a writing deadline but I'm procrastinating, I allow myself to knit in front of the television during business hours. If I'm putting off crocheting a sweater for my niece, I might research an article I'm writing. As long as I can keep

Getting Unstuck

Stuck is a state we all find ourselves in at one time or another, whether it's a major creative crisis or just feeling stymied by a task at work. Tomes have been written about what leads to such blocks, and even more tomes have been written about how to get unblocked.

"If I'm feeling like I don't have the answer to a creative task," Noah Scalin told me, "I usually just switch to something else and let the gears in the back of my mind keep turning on it. I'm a master creative procrastinator! I get tons of things done, just not the thing that I should be working on. Then I don't feel guilty about not doing the work, and eventually, I have no choice but to work on it."

Noah is an artist and designer, and author of the book *Unstuck*. His Skull-A-Day project was instrumental in popularizing the make-a-thing-every-day trend, and he routinely speaks to groups about creativity.

Fiber artist Sonya Philip takes a similar approach to procrastinating productively. "If I'm working on a piece that's very intricate, I'll turn to something simple and more free-form." With several projects in progress at any point, she always has something a little different to turn to when one thing becomes too much.

In fact, many people I've spoken to about procrastination tell me they take a similar approach. Do you? Can you?

We'll focus more on block and procrastination in Part Three (where you'll also see Noah and Sonya again, in the context of undertaking a daily project).

myself from falling into a rut that's utterly unproductive, I can keep the procrastination demons from derailing my creative life.

> **"When I realize I've been staring at a blank page for ten minutes, or that I've spent two hours in a Twitter-Tumblr-Facebook-Instagram K-hole, I think about all of the productive things I could have done with that time."**
>
> —ANN FRIEDMAN, JOURNALIST

Block

There's a fine line between block and procrastination. Block is the feeling of being unable to create, and procrastination is the putting-off of creation. Block feels like an external barrier, and procrastination is one that comes from within (even if we don't procrastinate *on purpose*).

This means that, to some extent, we can predict when we'll procrastinate, but we don't have it so easy when it comes to anticipating block. Block ambushes us, and because we don't see it coming, we can feel quite helpless.

The thing to remember is that block is not unusual, and it's not an indication of weakness. Sometimes it's the result of your brain being under siege by major demons, and sometimes it's just because you're tired or burnt out. I've felt blocked for hours, days, and occasionally weeks. It always ends. Always. Sometimes I can even help it along, and much of Part Four is dedicated to approaches to doing just that.

NAME THE DEMONS

FEAR OF FAILURE   SELF-DOUBT   PERFECTIONISM

PROCRASTINATION   BLOCK

In the last exercise, you listened hard to your ugly voice and wrote down what it says to you. Now we're going to look at those utterances to see what we can learn.

Go back to Speech Bubbles and examine what your ugly voice says to you. In the same way you used highlighters or crayons to get to the heart of your strengths in Section One, try to identify which major demon is saying each thing. Can you further identify which minor demon each utterance spawns? USE THE FOLLOWING PAGES TO MAKE NOTES OR DIAGRAMS TO HELP MAKE SENSE OF WHAT YOU FIND.

Are there things that don't directly correspond to a demon, but to an experience you've had in the past, to more tangible fears that plague you, to a person who's cut you down? Mark these issues, and see if you can draw lines between those experiences and the demons. You may find yourself in a chicken-and-egg game, trying to figure out whether something the ugly voice says is the cause of the demon, or whether a demon is what's spurring your ugly voice on. Don't worry about which came first—it's the examination itself that's the point here.

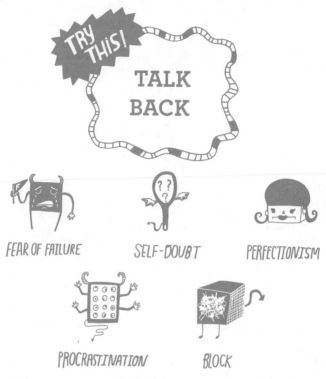

TRY THIS!

TALK BACK

FEAR OF FAILURE   SELF-DOUBT   PERFECTIONISM

PROCRASTINATION   BLOCK

Now. Here's a fresh set of speech bubbles. I want you to answer your ugly voice, talk back to the fears and trends and people you identified in the last exercise. Do it any way you'd like—all caps, drawings, stickers, paint, gorgeous cursive. The only rule is that you cannot, under any circumstances, agree with the ugly voice. If you're inclined to see the ugly voice's point, come up with a "but" statement and write down only that. Like only write down the bold part of this: "I see why you think I'm a spoiled brat, but I'll remind you that **I ALWAYS DROP EVERYTHING WHEN MY FRIENDS NEED ME.**"

When you're done, take a step back and admire your work. You've just fought your first battle against the demon horde.

Time for ice cream.

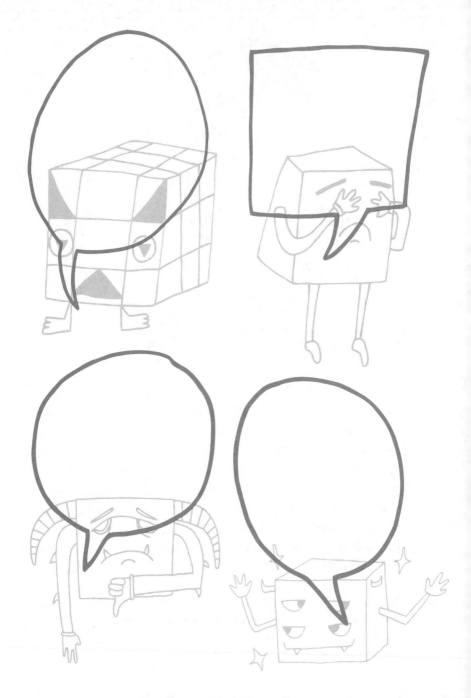

AND THEN I FELL OFF A CLIFF

A year and a half after I started working at *Interweave Crochet*, I spent about a week in bliss. I felt, for the first time, that I knew my job, like deep-down-in-my-bones knew it. I was at the top of the learning curve, which was squarely situated, obviously, on top of the world. People had questions? I had answers! It was fantastic.

The next week, I descended that dramatic slope into the most terrible rut I've faced in my adult life. Without knowing what hit me, I found myself mentally paralyzed. My brain felt foggy, if not entirely clouded over. I lost all excitement for my job. I felt incapable of returning e-mails or adhering to our production schedule. It was as if I were floating facedown, and I couldn't even flail my way to the occasional breath.

BAM!

(**SPOILER ALERT**: This was rock bottom for me, like from the J.K. Rowling quote back in the introduction. I didn't know it at the time, of course, but looking back, that rock bottom ended up serving as the solid foundation I've built myself back up from. This is when I started battling my demons.)

I was crushed. I was embarrassed. I was ashamed. I was stressed out. I was blocked. My inability to work transcended procrastination and entered the realm of negligence. I was uninterested in making stuff, even on my own time.

Eventually, I started taking shots in the dark in a desperate attempt to hit some sort of effective target. I rented a desk in a shared office for a change of scenery. I adopted productivity recipes: to-do lists based on one or another ideology, this or another app to organize my ideas (ideas I wasn't having), notebooks, color-coding.

Nothing worked for very long, if it worked at all, and my continued inability to get it together made me feel even worse. What had I been thinking, taking this job? Why did I think this job would be different from any other job I'd had? I'd hated everything I'd ever done before, so why should this be different? Why was *I* so different? Other people would love my job! It was a fabulous job! Hell, other people can do their job even if they don't love it! They go to work every day anyway, sometimes for years and decades! They don't need stupid color-coded to-do list systems just to get them out of bed in the morning!

I had failed. I had failed to love the job anyone else in their right mind would love. I had failed to do the job properly. I was letting down the people I worked with, and the people who had come to look to me for ideas and creativity and leadership in my field. I was finally showing my true colors as a fraud, and clearly there was nothing for me to do but admit defeat and sit on my couch for a few months trying to figure out how to spend the next fifty years of my life as an unemployable, lazy sot who couldn't follow through to finish even the most straightforward of tasks.

Here's some of what I figured out during this time, when I was forced to pull myself together and I could only manage to do it if I flipped my entire perception of myself around:

> My inability to finish projects? A strength in *starting* projects. (Also, let's keep in mind that I'd written five books at this point. All mostly done on time! I could finish projects.)

> My fickle attention? I get bored easily and need to plan accordingly.

> The stomachaches I was suffering? I was bored and needed to move on; I've learned to listen to what my body tells me.

I decided to quit my dream job. I didn't quit because I still felt defeated. And I didn't still feel broken, like I couldn't do what everyone else in the world does without hesitation. And I didn't feel weak.

I quit my job because I had to deal with the boredom and the burnout. And my decision to leave the magazine afforded me the opportunity to keep an open mind when the company I was leaving wanted to buy Crochet Me. It took some very hard convincing, and a lot of negotiation, for me to decide my baby would be treated properly. And when I finally felt it would be, I solved my problems by being able to walk away from crochet entirely for a while.

After two years at the magazine, we announced that I was leaving and that I was selling the website. I knew I was making the right decision—my stomachaches were gone, my block was gone, my mind was clear—but I was certain no one else would understand. Though I'd battled the demons of my own self-perception (I'd followed the block demons back up the chain to self-doubt and the shame of fearing I was failing because I was a freak), I was still quite confident that as far as other people were concerned, I was a lazy-oaf quitter. I still wasn't sure my boss understood (though her response when I'd told her a few months earlier—a chortle about working with creative people—hinted that she did), and I was certain my readers and fans wouldn't. I was certain they'd feel personally slighted, like my quitting was insulting them. I was certain they'd feel let down, like their cheerleader was abandoning the cause. I was certain they'd judge me like I'd judged myself since I was a teenager, like I was a flighty flake who couldn't commit or follow through.

I wrote a blog post explaining my decision, and I was terrified to hit "publish." I braced myself for a firestorm of hate.

As it turned out, I received only supportive blog comments, and some downright touching e-mails from people who also felt like freaks for not wanting what's "normal." I ended up being interviewed by podcasters I really admired. And I ended up strengthening friendships with people I'd had no idea felt the same way, themselves. For all my anxiety about being misunderstood and judged harshly, I ended up falling into a pile of support that enabled me to fully enjoy my decisions and make tremendous strides in accepting being a freak.

This grand adventure is what led me directly into the arms of Mighty Ugly just a couple of years later. All my fear of being misunderstood, my shame about being different, how stuck I felt about what to do next—I piled it all together and started making ugly things. The more I thought about ugliness, the more excited I became about beauty. The more I accepted my failures and failings, the more confident I felt about trying new things. The more I spoke with other people about how I felt, the more comfortable I became because I wasn't alone.

Now, I just do what I want to do. When I don't feel like knitting for four months, I no longer browbeat myself—I just don't knit. When a fabulous opportunity shows up on my doorstep, but it's a long-term commitment I don't think I'll end up wanting to complete, I don't take it, and I force myself to ignore the ugly voice that tells me I'm being irresponsible or ungrateful. I say back to it, "It's irresponsible to set myself up to let people down and to make myself miserable. Go fix yourself a maggot sandwich, ugly voice. I got this."

LOCUS OF CONTROL

There's a psychological theory that's applied to how individuals attribute causation in their own experiences. At the extremes, people with an *internal locus of control* believe they have a very high degree of control over their experiences, whereas people with an *external locus of control* believe their experiences are controlled almost entirely by environmental factors or other people.

Naturally, there's a vast sea of gray between these extremes, but you can probably think of people you know who have exhibited a maddening display at one extreme or another. Maybe a coworker believes every snag she encounters is the result of her being inept, or a friend complains over a plate of bacon that his doctor says he's not trying hard enough to improve his diet. To the former, you insist over and over again that there are a dozen other factors that influenced her setback and that she's great at her job and very capable; to the latter, you raise an eyebrow and wonder if he ever takes responsibility for his own actions.

I find it very helpful to think about this theory when examining my creative struggles. Am I being too hard on myself, dismissing valid external factors that contributed to my failure? Maybe my article submission wasn't rejected because my writing was terrible, but rather because the editor was focusing on a different topic. Or am I defensively blaming something else instead of accepting that I screwed up? Maybe my quilt is wonky not so much because the blade of my rotary cutter was loose, but because I measured wrong.

This is relevant to success, too. I can't stand it when people attribute their successes to luck—it's unfair to themselves, and it's falsely humble. At the same time, I do think it's important to acknowledge the role that privilege and happenstance play in our successes. Taking an honest look at what contributes to our successes can be just as difficult as doing the same for our failures, and it's just as important for our growing ability to handle both in stride.

TRY THIS!

LOCUS OF CONTROL

FEAR OF FAILURE   **SELF-DOUBT**   **PERFECTIONISM**

Think about a couple of recent projects you've completed—one a failure and one a success. Feel free to use apples and oranges here—the success could be from work and the failure from pottery class, doesn't matter. Try to remember how you talked about each—did you indicate to your partner or a friend that you were responsible for the outcome, or that you were a victim of external forces, or something in between?

Were you fair in your assessment? If you were, right on. If you weren't, what have you learned that you might apply the next time around?

It's always advisable to avoid extremes. If you find you're beating yourself up about a project you're working on, step back and look to see if you're being *too* hard on yourself. Do the same if you find you're in a rage about how someone or something has completely ruined your life. Any chance you played some part in it? Try hard to reach some sort of middle ground, which is a good place to stand when you need to figure out what's happened and what to do next.

"A few years ago I went back to school for graphic design, and during that time I saw the demand for my artwork increase tenfold. It was a huge confidence booster for me to be fielding gallery show invites and commercial illustration jobs all while juggling a full time intensive design program, so I agreed to everything that came my way. Suddenly the little puddle I was hopping around in turned into a struggle to keep my head above water in this new flash flood of demand. I hung up a few pieces of my artwork for a group show, and at the opening my good friend, who sugarcoats nothing, turned to me and said, "Definitely not your best work. Did you run out of time?" As much as it stung, it was so true. I let my blind over-scheduling dilute the quality of my work, and it truly showed."

—STACEY ROZICH, ARTIST

Skewed Perspective

Lauren Bacon is an author, tech entrepreneur, and business coach who writes frequently about women in tech and her own experiences taking risks in business. I asked her to tell me about trends she's noticed in how people deal with their creative demons in the business world, and she brought up this issue of the locus of control.

"One of the big demons I see among entrepreneurs is going to extremes around how personally to take failure. Some people take it completely to heart, as though all the responsibility for the failure lies somewhere within them, and others blame it all on outside circumstances, without taking time to reflect on what they could have done differently. In the former case, you're neglecting to look realistically on what external factors contribute to the success or failure of your venture, and in the latter, you've missed an opportunity to learn and grow from your mistakes. Either way, it's a very skewed way of looking at things."

Lauren mentioned the economic downturn of 2008 as a great example. Lots of businesses, including her own at the time, struggled in the wake of the recession. For some business owners, it may have been tempting to blame themselves for not weathering the storm more successfully; for others, the new economic climate made for an easy scapegoat. As with most things, taking a moderate approach is often the sensible thing to do—learn from the hardship and adapt accordingly. The same applies to less dire circumstances, say, at your dining room table with a bunch of art supplies spread out in front of you.

SECTION 3: MIGHTY UGLY

TRY THIS!

MIGHTY UGLY

FEAR OF FAILURE   SELF-DOUBT   PERFECTIONISM

PROCRASTINATION   BLOCK

Put this book down right now and take a deep breath, then pick it back up. You made it through the tough part, through the uncomfortable thoughts and feelings, and my insistence that slogging through was for your own good.

Now it's time to put the knowledge you gleaned to good use.

You've reached the Mighty Ugly exercise, the one that started me on this adventure. I'm hoping it'll start you on an adventure, too. Use it as a springboard into the rest of the book, eh?

First things first. I think this exercise is fun. Then again, I've done it lots of times and you've probably never done it. So you may not think it's fun. You may find it daunting, confusing, intimidating, or even threatening. You may find it easy, liberating, or even profound. You may roll your eyes and wonder what the big deal is. You may feel and think any number of those things or countless other things. All good.

You do not need to show the ugly creature you're about to make to anyone, but you're welcome to.* You can throw it away in the end, or you can keep it. Name it, or butcher it, or both. Your choice.

Here we go.

⬇ ⬇ ⬇

EXERCISE, PART ONE

First, gather some materials you can use to make a creature. Anything will do, and even better if you use scraps or trash or other doodads you won't miss and don't find precious. Some possibilities:

* scrap fabric and/or yarn
* bottle caps

----

* We live in the internet age! If you decide to share a photo of your creature online, tag it #mightyugly! And if you want to share your experience of making it, tag your post or tweet (or whatever new kind of sharing thing that doesn't even exist yet when I'm writing this)—tag it #mightyugly. And if you want to tell me about it, shoot me a tweet at @kpwerker or an e-mail at kim@mightyugly.com.

* twist ties
* leftover beads
* wood scraps
* wire cuttings
* cardboard boxes
* paint
* markers
* pipe cleaners
* twine
* packaging materials

You'll need some tools too. Whatever you have on hand, like:

* scissors
* glue (a glue gun works fastest, if you have one)
* tape
* stapler
* wire cutter
* sewing needle and thread

Make sure you have enough time to do the exercise in one sitting. Set aside a minimum of an hour, but give yourself a limit—you need to be done in ninety minutes, no more.

Now, make an ugly creature. Those are the only two criteria: 1) Ugly. 2) Creature.

Do not make your creature cute-ugly. Make it ugly-ugly. Not the kind of ugly that engenders compassion, but the kind that inspires revulsion. Before you start, take some time to think about what ugly is.

You may find that, as you construct your creature, you need to change direction to stop making it look cute, pretty, or just vaguely good. You may need to change direction more than once. One of the key purposes of this exercise is to keep you focused on the process of making something rather than on the product you'll end up with at the end.

While you make the creature, keep in mind the demons you've identified. Don't try to conjure them, necessarily, but try to notice when they start quietly infiltrating your ranks. Certainly notice them if they outright attack. Pause for a sec—what are you thinking or doing when the demons show up? When is it that you start to think you're bound to fail? How are you defining failure in that moment—is it about making something ugly or pretty (it's intentionally confusing in this context!)? When do you feel blocked? When do you fret that you won't be able to make the creature perfect in the allotted time? When are you convinced you never should have tried this in the first place?

OK, enough from me.

Go! Make an ugly creature! Come back here when you're done.

FLIP IT AROUND: OK, fine. In the same amount of time, make a beautiful creature. Compare and contrast your experience of doing it this way with doing it the ugly way.

EXERCISE, PART TWO

Now that you've made your creature, write out its story. What are its quirks? Does its personality fit how ugly it is on the outside, or is it beautiful on the inside (or uglier)? Sinister? Is it a do-gooder? What was its childhood like? What are its dreams and aspirations?

When I lead Mighty Ugly workshops, I find that about half the participants concoct a story while they're making their creature, and about half are dumbfounded when I ask them for a story. So, if you're in the latter group, you're not alone, and this part of the exercise might be the hardest part. That's OK. Make it up; there's no wrong answer.

BONUS EXERCISE: Send me your story with a snapshot of your creature at kim@mightyugly.com. And if you feel like it, tell me what you think of this exercise now that you've done it.

EXERCISE, PART THREE

Consider some questions.

When I was making my ugly creature, I felt:
a. silly
b. challenged
c. uncomfortable
d. threatened
e. relieved

My creature is ugly because:
a. It's grotesque.
b. The colors don't match.
c. It's ill-shapen and/or asymmetrical.
d. It makes me uncomfortable.
e. It's evil.

To make my creature ugly, I had to:
a. deliberately make it not match, make it not symmetrical
b. remember what it was like to make stuff when I was a kid
c. choose colors I don't like
d. think of what kinds of personality traits I find ugly
e. do the opposite of what I usually do when I make stuff

Does your creature have a name? While you were making it, did you think about any of the demons or ugly-voice utterances you dug up earlier in this section? What did you notice? Were you able to quiet those influences? How does your experience making something ugly relate to your experience of making something in general—were you hard on yourself? Easy? Did you notice any perfectionist inclinations? Did you doubt you could do it? Were you afraid of ending up with something cute or pretty?

How does your experience making something ugly on purpose affect how you think about other projects you do at work or for fun? How does it make you feel about projects you fantasize about doing?

Keep these things in mind as you progress through the book. You've done the hardest work. The rest will help you fight, and maybe even slay, your demons. It'll be hard, but not as hard as being honest enough with yourself to name them. And it'll be way more fun.

F. U., MRS. O.

My friend Miranda glued a pipe cleaner to the body of her ugly creature not by putting glue between the pipe cleaner and the body, but
by draping glue over the top of the pipe cleaner like a strap. When
she introduced her creature to the other people sitting around a
table in my living room the very first time I led a Mighty Ugly workshop, she told a story from when she was in the first grade. Her class
was making dioramas—creating "naturescapes" in cardboard boxes
with leaves and twigs and stuff they'd collected outside. Miranda
couldn't get the problematic surface texture of a pinecone to cooper-
ate with the glue, and in a moment of inspiration decided to use the
glue differently, draping it over the pinecone like a strap. It worked,
and the next day her teacher held up her diorama in front of the class
as an example of how not to use glue. Over twenty years later,
Miranda named her ugly creature "F. U., Mrs. O."*

----

* I first told a version of Miranda's story in a segment for *Longshot Radio* in
2012. *Longshot* is a whole radio show that's made from start to finish in just
in forty-eight hours. This episode was on the topic of creativity and failure.
Listen at bit.ly/longshotradio.

SO HERE WE ARE. Welcome to creative life with a head full of demons and an ugly voice that shouts at you loud and clear.

You just did some very important work, and I'm proud of you for sticking it out. I hope you're proud of you too. I promise that very few of the exercises in the rest of the book will involve such deep introspection. Instead, we'll focus on using your newfound knowledge of your creative demons to help you start making stuff. Or, if you already make stuff, to help you make more stuff and have more fun doing it.

We'll explore what I mean when I talk about the power of *embracing* creative demons. Oh, we'll fight some demons too, for sure. But we'll also try to give some a hug, or at least a fist bump, because we'll learn to get comfortable knowing that our demons can be good for us sometimes.

Our demons can help us see the future, by serving as powerful predictors of our creative experiences (they can help us sense when we'll end up happy and when we'll end up miserable). And they can help us remember the past, by nagging us about mistakes we'd do well to correct. And they can help us travel through space and time by giving us some of those woo-woo intuitions that tell us when to stay the course and when to about-face and when to put a project down for a week or a year.

The theme of this section? **DO IT.** Do it even if you're certain you won't enjoy it. Do it even if you don't know how. Fail spectacularly, and then do it again. Don't worry about it, don't talk yourself out of it, try not to care if what you make is awful—just make.

SECTION 1: YOU'RE CREATIVE, LET'S MAKE SOMETHING

The Snowball Effect

My friend Rachael Ashe is a photographer and paper artist who creates breathtaking altered books and cut-paper works. She wields a knife like I only wish I could wield a pencil. In 2013, I attended a talk she gave about the trajectory that took her from working as a photographer to being a full-time maker. She described identifying that the transition of her photography from film-based to digital had left a void in her creative life—her work was no longer hands-on.

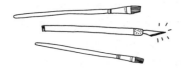

She started to make altered books, and then she signed up to participate in The Sketchbook Project. Participants in the project are sent a blank sketchbook, which they're charged to fill up in whatever way they'd like, and then send back. The project has well over 30,000 sketchbooks in its collection. Anyone can participate, from writers to photographers to people like Rachael, looking for a nudge to explore their creativity.

Rachael explains, "Exploring collage was my gateway to hands-on making, and it allowed me to develop previously untapped skills of working with paper materials, and creating from a place of play." Participating in The Sketchbook Project gave Rachael a defined timeline and end goal (two things we'll explore more in Part Three). "It's something I could do in a limited time frame and set specific parameters around what I wanted to achieve. I had a Moleskine sketchbook I used as my focus, and made one collage a week in this. Even at the start, I was anticipating the end result of a bulging sketchbook full of collage work."

"I think collage is accessible to people who think they aren't creative because there is no right or wrong way to do it. Stick two pieces of paper (or even one) onto a third piece of paper or some sort of canvas, and you have a collage." Keep making collages and you get better and better at it.

So this is where we're going to start making stuff.

The Sketchbook Project exhibits its collection at its library in Brooklyn, NY; across North America in its Mobile Library; and online in its Digital Library. Peruse the collection and sign up to participate at www.sketchbookproject.com.

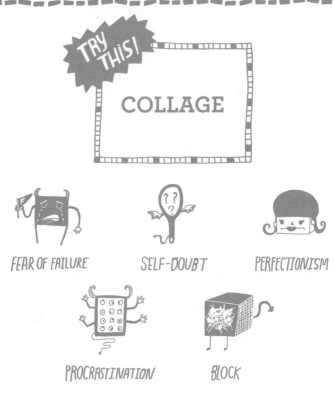

TRY THIS!

COLLAGE

FEAR OF FAILURE   SELF-DOUBT   PERFECTIONISM

PROCRASTINATION   BLOCK

Make a collage. Gather up the handful of magazines you have stashed around your house because you'll read them someday, and some scissors and glue or tape. Cut up the magazines, and make a pile of images that appeal to you. Give yourself a special challenge, if you want, like to only use cut-out faces or landscape elements, or to focus on a particular color or other kind of theme. Add in other sorts of stuff if you're so inclined—found objects, receipts, ticket stubs, buttons—and stick it all to a piece of cardboard (a panel from a cereal box is great for this, or just use a scrap piece of paper—the thicker the better, especially if you're using found objects that can be a bit heavy for paper to support). Play around until you're happy with it. Step away whenever you need a break.

FLIP IT AROUND: There will certainly be moments when you feel dissatisfied with the state of your collage—pause for a sec and think about why. Is it the look of it? Is it a demon or your ugly voice getting in your way? Try to fight back. Remember your hero qualities. Your demons are not the boss of you, and you are the boss of this collage. Try to notice the difference between your aesthetic sense not being satisfied (because the colors are clashing or the overall look of your composition is wonky) and being under attack. Take a deep breath and continue gluing anyway. Your demons will suffer a blow simply through your continued act of making.

Tim Brown, CEO of design firm IDEO, gave a TED talk in 2008 about how designers use play as a way to "unselfconsciously surrender themselves." I find his whole talk inspiring, especially because we adults could certainly do a whole lot more playing, even at work: bit.ly/creativity-play.

I DIDN'T THINK I WAS CREATIVE, EITHER

One afternoon when I was a grad student in my early twenties, I sat slumped in my statistics professor's office. I was a year into studying for my PhD, doing just fine in his class and in the others I was taking. By all accounts, I should have been on a honeymoon of academic success, but I was utterly miserable. And I just could not figure out why.

I remember talking and talking to my professor but feeling like I wasn't saying what I wanted to say. I was trying to express how I'd realized I needed a creative outlet. I was restless and unhappy and I felt like I was living a life that wasn't the one I wanted, despite my successes. I knew all about what I didn't want to be doing—for one, following along with the status quo just because that's the way things were always done—and I had no idea where to start to figure out what I did want to do.

I needed a hobby. I felt a deep-down craving to make stuff. I was so sure I needed this that I was overwhelmed by desperation. I felt like if I didn't find a creative outlet soon, I'd stop being able to cope, full stop.

Part of my confusion stemmed from the nagging fact that I'd never actually had a hobby. I mean, I used to read lots of books in my free time (and still do), but that wasn't creative. I wanted to express myself, and I had no idea how.

I was twenty-three and utterly ignorant about what creative people did, and I was sure I was too old to ever learn. Creative people are born creative, I knew, and I was not creative. I lacked that *je ne sais quoi*, and I was so painfully aware of it that I couldn't stand it, and I couldn't stand myself.

Creative people draw well and can sing and act and dance. They've done these things since they were small, obviously. Sometimes they have blue hair. And awesome boots. They date poets and nihilists. They have talent and panache. They know how to party, and their homes are gorgeous shrines to aesthetics and art, and cool music I've never heard of is always playing in the background.

> **"Everyone is creative in some way, not just artists. Artists just seem more creative because they spend a large amount of their time cultivating it. People need to go through the process of trying different things in order to figure out where their creative strengths lie."**
>
> —RACHAEL ASHE, ARTIST

I was a great student when I was younger, at times gregarious and at times painfully shy, and I felt untethered and misunderstood about almost everything outside the classroom, and especially about this void I felt that I was sure could be filled by being creative, if only I knew how. If only I'd been born that way and knew the cool music and felt brave enough to wear awesome boots and paint stripes on my bedroom wall.

Eventually, I just went to a big-box craft store and wandered around for a long time. I couldn't draw or paint. Or sculpt. Or knit. Or sew. The desperation of my quest left me needing instant gratification lest I perish right there in the fake-flower aisle, and I wandered from section to section until I found a kit to make mosaic coasters.

Aha!

I wouldn't need to be good at drawing or painting, and I wouldn't even need to pick colors. And I'd learn how to grout, an arguably practical skill!

I brought the kit home, and my then-not-yet-boyfriend (an engineer, not a nihilist) and I followed the instructions to the letter, and wouldn't you know, we ended up with tiled coasters. They weren't Picassos, but they were level enough to hold a mug without spilling, which was all I needed for encouragement. We enjoyed it all so much we decided to make more mosaics, but for real this time.

We bought a tile scorer and went to town in the bathroom-tile section of Home Depot. We got some plywood boards to use as canvases and got to work. I sketched and re-sketched the turtle I wanted to make from the pile of green and yellow tiles I bought.*

In the time it took me to start filling in the turtle's shell with my imperfectly cut tile pieces, my then-not-yet-boyfriend had tiled and grouted a three-by-four-foot desert landscape. This gave me pause.

In the years since, my now-husband has created works of mosaic art that continue to take my breath away.

I never finished the turtle.

It was a familiar frustration—not to be able to translate what I saw in my head into any sort of tangible form. Again, I was left with the certainty that I simply was not creative. My misery persisted. I had some very strong, well-trained creative demons to battle, but it was another couple of years before they drove me to the impulsive, dramatic act that seemed like rock bottom but was really a major turning point.

In Part One, you identified and started to stare down your creative demons. Now you're ready to engage them in some light battle. Perhaps the most important thing to do at this early stage is to get yourself into shape. On the following pages, you'll find ideas and exercises that will help you build up your creative muscles, so you can start to deal those demons some damage.

OK, FINE: ACCEPTING MY CREATIVITY

About a year after the mosaic-turtle-desert-landscape incident, my restlessness led me to leave grad school to take a job running an after-school program at a community center. I felt I needed to work in the so-called "real world" since I'd always been a student, and I felt a strong desire to contribute to society.

----

* I had decided a year earlier to try to fill a different void in my life by having turtles as my "thing." I'd never even properly met a turtle. To this day I don't know a thing about them, except that I have a few figurines leftover from my wayward early twenties.

It was the worst job I ever had, but I'm very glad I spent a year doing it. The stresses, frustrations, and challenges I felt on a daily basis—especially on top of the amorphous discomfort I continued to feel even after I'd left grad school—led me to finally do the right thing for myself. It was impulsive and, some might argue, irresponsible. But I felt backed into a corner and couldn't see any other way to try to feel better.

I quit that job without a plan. I just couldn't take it anymore.

And I learned right quick that normal people don't do things like that. My mother gasped into the phone, "What will you do about health insurance?!" Friends received the news with thin lips, trying hard to hide their shock.

It was the first time I realized I'm, for real, not "normal." Behaving abnormally was the first time I felt pure happiness as a young adult. Or, scratch that: **FINALLY NOT FORCING MYSELF TO BEHAVE NORMALLY IS WHAT MADE ME FEEL HAPPY.** I'd been holding back for so long.

I didn't know then that this realization was the only thing I needed to get in touch with my creative self. A kit from the craft store wasn't going to unlock that achievement.

It was the first time I wasn't terribly bothered that people judged my actions, because I knew that what I had done was right. It didn't need to be right for them; it needed to be right for me.

The last thing I had to do for my job, which involved running the community center's summer travel camp for teens, was to take a group of ten fifteen-year-old girls on a seventeen-day trip around the American Southwest. It was tremendous fun, and at the end of the trip, after I'd dropped the kids off at the airport, I had to drive our rental van from San Francisco to Phoenix by myself.

My only responsibility was to arrive in Phoenix in time to have dinner with my cousins before they took the van and me to the airport for my flight back east. All told, I drove about sixteen hours over two days, and spoke to no one, apart from the clerk at a cheap motel in Bakersfield.

Somewhere in the middle of the desert, during about hour seven of thinking (and panicking) about my job situation, I realized I was going to be just fine. I'd find a temp job as a stopgap,* but beyond that I'd really just be fine. I felt it in my bones. I felt that for the first time, I was in charge of my life. And since I was in charge, I was finally able to see myself as worthy of exploration.

That drive, fraught with intense worry and then the freedom of catharsis, was the first and last time I've ever enjoyed being in the desert.**

In her commencement address to the 2012 graduating class at Gettysburg College, Jacqueline Novogratz included this quote from the poet Rilke:

"Try to love the questions themselves, as if they were locked rooms or books written in a foreign language. Don't search for the answers, which could not be given to you now, because you would not be able to live them. And the point is to live everything. Live the questions now. Perhaps then, someday far in the future, you will gradually, without even noticing it, live your way into the answer."

Watch her whole address at bit.ly/novogratz-gettysburg.

----

* In the state of Delaware at the time, substitute teachers worked through a temp agency. Yes, I have tales to tell. And yes, you can buy me a drink and I'll shower you with them.
** I really and truly hate the desert. I always feel funny in a place that's perpetually sunny and dry. Not funny like a clown. Funny like my organs aren't functioning properly.

THE GREAT UNKNOWN

In his book *Uncertainty*, Jonathan Fields writes about creative people who have an exceptionally high tolerance for, you guessed it, uncertainty. This tolerance enables them to take dramatic risks less comfortable people wouldn't even consider as possible options. I didn't think, when I quit my job, that I was being creative, but I would eventually learn that it takes a heckuva lot of comfort with the unknown to quit a job without a plan. And though it's rarely the right decision to do such a thing, when it is the right decision, it's right to such a dramatic extent that the results of following through with it can be downright profound.

Which is not to imply that after I quit my job, my whole life fell into place, and I lived happily ever after. I'd have gotten to happy a lot more quickly if I'd identified, at the time, that taking a big risk and coming up with solutions to the problems I'd created for myself exemplified the type of creative person I am. (This is my favorite way to make things, now—I just go go go until I've gotten myself into a horrible tangle; in the untangling, I find answers, and the satisfaction that comes with them.)

In fact, it wasn't until I finally figured out and, importantly, accepted that I am creative, that my baby steps turned into giant leaps toward chilling out and enjoying my life. I learned, and then eventually accepted, that creativity does not manifest itself only through the fine arts. I learned that figuring out how to make my first decrease in a knitting project when I'd forgotten to bring the instructions with me on an airplane takes creativity. I learned that figuring out how to make that decrease on my own empowered me to see my stitches in a whole new way; it enabled me to know I could manipulate them however I want. I learned and accepted that manipulating everyday things in new ways is itself a creative exercise. I eventually realized that I've expressed myself creatively my whole life, not through art but through words. Recognizing that I'm a writer was perhaps the most profound, absurdly obvious event of my adult life.

Talk of creativity is often limited to the realms of visual art, writing, crafts, performing arts, etc., but creativity plays an invaluable role in every sort of endeavor, from the science lab to the boardroom to the classroom. If you're inclined to insist you're not creative, give some thought to this. Think about problems you routinely solve at work; think about that challenging nook in your kitchen and how you run through ideas for how to make the best of it; think about the last family kerfuffle you were stuck in the middle of, and how you tried your best to be diplomatic and mend fences. All of these seemingly mundane tasks involve creativity. They all involve figuring out how to use the tools and skills and materials at hand to solve a problem. Keep this in mind the next time you're about to insist you're not creative. Give yourself the credit you're due, and remember that creativity is what sets humans apart from lizards.

SECTION 2: MISTAKES & SQUIRMING! THEY'RE SO GREAT!

A CARDBOARD ROBOT

Sometimes, I think of Mighty Ugly as an opportunity—or a challenge—to insert some childhood back into adulthood. Whenever I speak with people in my workshops or just in general about creativity and why making ugly things is so great, inevitably childhood comes up. After we recall how much fun we had making popsicle-stick houses and clay pots, we move on to produce at least one memory of an event or conversation that chipped away at our youthful creative abandon—but we recall that creative abandon fondly, as if it were a school friend who moved far away, whom we never saw again.

If you're raising your eyebrows at my assertion that we all had creative abandon as children, come on. Of course you did too. If not expressed through crayons and finger paint, then maybe it came out in tales of make-believe, duels of sticks and mud, skits at family reunions, songs in the bathtub, dance routines to Top 40 hits on the radio. And I'd bet money that if you take a hard look back, you'll come up with a memory of the souring of one or another of your creative expressions. Maybe it was a friend or cousin poking fun at you; an adult, hopefully well-meaning, steering you to an activity he or she thought better suited you; a comment from a teacher; a self-assessed failure or feeling of frustration. And after that, it became a part of your identity, in some small or large way: you don't or can't do that thing.

Before I started second grade, I was terrified of Ms. Ancona, who would be my teacher. She had a reputation for yelling. She had a lot of energy. I could see this from my perspective as a first grader with a very mild-mannered teacher. I cried before the first day of second grade.

In that perverse manner of childhood, I ended up adoring my second-grade teacher. Yes, she yelled. And she was energetic. And due to those qualities and others, her smiles were worth more than gold, and she challenged me in all the best of ways.

In one of my most vivid memories of the year I was seven, I'm standing on a chair at the back of the classroom. It's possible I'm even standing on a desk, heresy of heresies. I needed to stand so high because I was several weeks (possibly days, pesky immature memory) into constructing a cardboard robot. I don't recall the purpose of this project, nor the topic of study it was related to. I just remember the irreverent bliss of standing on that chair/desk juxtaposed against my fretting over the state of my robot. It was not doing what I wanted it to do; it did not look how I envisioned it in my mind. No matter how I tried or what I tried or for how long, it did not get better. My bliss from standing up so high eroded in the face of my failure. The robot was an engineering catastrophe, and because I had such trouble keeping the whole thing together, I never achieved the fun of immersing myself in the absurdity of making it.

I don't usually lean toward perfectionism, but boy, was I defeated by it over my cardboard robot. I don't remember what happened to that thing, or if I even received marks for the project. My memory doesn't involve anyone but me, and my failure to execute the elaborate vision I'd concocted. After that project, I was less willing to take on audacious challenges, because I was less confident in my ability to execute them.

What if I could go back? What if we all could go back? What if we could undo the lessons we've learned about how hard it can be to make stuff, and overwrote them with lessons about how fun it is to try? I mean, can't it be enough to delight in just having permission to stand on the table? Can't it be enough to spend a few hours with tape and cardboard and our infinite imaginations?

I think it can. I don't think we've lost our childhood wonder forever. Maybe we've hidden it behind our mental filing cabinets filled with taxes and medical records and gas bills, but we can dig it out. It's not immature or irresponsible to do so. It might just be the thing we need to have more fun and make more stuff.

One day in 2011, filmmaker Nirvan Mullick stopped into a Los Angeles car-parts shop to pick up a door handle, and stumbled upon the owner's nine-year-old son and the cardboard arcade he'd spent the summer building. The resulting short film, *Caine's Arcade*, went viral several months later, and people from all over the world who were touched by the story donated in excess of a couple hundred thousand dollars to establish a college fund for Caine, and Nirvan founded a non-profit called the Imagination Foundation, dedicated to fostering children's imagination, play, and invention. Caine and Nirvan have traveled near and far, speaking with kids and adults, teachers and business titans about the power of fostering kids' imaginations using materials as simple as cardboard and tape. Prepare to be inspired: bit.ly/caines-arcade-film.

"Mistakes and failures *are* my designs. I don't think I've ever created one design in my entire life that looks exactly like I originally envisioned it."

—BETSY CROSS, JEWELRY DESIGNER

THAT TIME I KNITTED A SAUNA

When I decided to make my first sweater about a year after I learned how to knit, I chose a very simple pattern in a bulky yarn. I treated myself with kid gloves, not wanting to discourage myself by trying something too far beyond my ability. I wanted some quick success.

After a few weeks of feverish knitting, I began to set the sleeves into the body of the sweater, and I immediately began to suspect I'd done something horribly wrong. This green yarn I'd chosen? Suddenly seemed to be made of lead. And it was very Kermit, if you know what I mean. Before even sewing up the sleeve seams, I pulled the half-assembled thing over my head and discovered that it weighed a hundred and fifty pounds and raised my body temperature forty degrees.

I was horrified. Mortified. Shocked.

I stared at that mostly completed sweater for a very long time. I tried it on a few more times too, in case time might fix all the problems.

In the end, I put it in the corner. It stayed in that corner for several years while I waited for physics to alter its laws to accommodate it. Eventually, I just ripped the whole thing out.

> **"I think a lot about that Ira Glass quote about how tough it is to be someone who consumes great work, and knows they're capable of making great work, but hasn't quite honed the skills yet. I expect most of my life to be spent in that middle ground—knowing I'm capable of greater things and trying not to hate myself because everything I've made so far hasn't been the GREATEST."**
>
> —ANN FRIEDMAN, JOURNALIST

> Ira Glass, host of US public-radio show *This American Life*, is a master storyteller and is very wise when it comes to the trials of starting something new. His own tales of starting out in journalism are inspiring if for no other reason than that he's very honest about how terrible he was, and he is outstanding now. About wanting to do good work but not quite being able to yet, he's said: "It's totally normal. And the most important possible thing you can do is do a lot of work." Watch him say it, along with other absolutely brilliant things, at bit.ly/iraglass-beginning.

OPTIMISM

Euphemisms drive me nuts, because I don't see why we shouldn't just call things what they are. When someone I love dies, I say they died. If a situation is not likely to turn out well, I'm not inclined to smile and say it'll all be fine. I don't believe we gain anything by pretending the seedy underbelly of the world doesn't exist. Reality deserves honesty.*

> Spend some time at www.craftfail.com perusing years' worth of spectacular craft failures contributed by intrepid crafters from around the world.

For these reasons, it came as a great shock when I discovered I'm an optimist. I'd been thinking about myself all wrong, it seems, by struggling to see the light in the world while I knew I wasn't a particularly shiny, happy person. A realist is what I thought of myself

---

* Yes, I also believe that fiction can sometimes illuminate reality better than reality itself.

as—not all doom and gloom like a pessimist, but certainly inclined to see the filthy, painful, ugly parts of life rather than to smile and cheerlead it all away.

It seems, though, that what makes an optimist is not shiny happiness, but a belief that things will turn out OK in the end, even if you acknowledge how terrible things are in the present. If there's one thing I believe, even in the face of crisis upon heartbreaking crisis, it's that it'll get better eventually. Not magically, but perhaps just in time and perhaps with a good deal of effort.

Optimism. Ugly can become beautiful. Failure can become success. Pain can become sweet relief.

My daily mantra is "I am an optimist." I'm still surprised by how effective it is for me to keep this in mind when the going gets tough.

DATE NIGHT

TRY THIS!

SELF-DOUBT   BLOCK

We have some kind of societal thing about loners. Maybe it's because we watched *Heathers* a few too many times when we were adolescents or something. We seem to assume that people out and about by themselves are to be pitied or avoided. Put yarn or thread or a book in their hand? Forget about it—loser central.

Aside from applying judgment for no good reason, a great downside to this attitude about loners is that we rarely go out alone ourselves. And by "going out," I don't mean running errands. I mean doing things we otherwise associate almost exclusively with being social—eating out, going to an amusement park, bowling, attending concerts or sporting events. We internalize the assumption that being alone makes us freaks. And feeling like a freak is part of why we struggle to figure out our creative desires, since being creative inherently involves *not doing exactly what everyone else is doing*.

I don't remember the first time I went to the movies by myself. I don't even remember when it was. I do remember feeling anxious about it, though, like people would notice me and know I'm a loser, even though I was out by myself by my own choosing. I think the reason I don't remember the details is that after the movie, I discovered what I'd always suspected to be true: it just doesn't matter if other people looked at me sideways. And also, I don't think anyone looked at me at all. Nobody really cared. Only I cared. And what was the point of worrying when I actually really enjoyed myself? I loved not having to coordinate plans with someone else. I loved not having to talk. I loved sitting through the end of the credits of whatever movie it was, then walking back to my car at my own pace. That night, the movies were more of an escape for me than they'd ever been, and I've been a habitual loner ever since.

Changing up the way we experience familiar activities, events, and settings can do more than open up an opportunity to combat self-doubt. It can also give us an easy-to-arrange, inexpensive adventure that can help break us out of a rut. Especially for introverts, who don't always feel refreshed after a night out with friends, a night out alone can be downright revolutionary.

You might not want to become a habitual public loner, but I do encourage you to be a freak.

⇩ ⇩ ⇧

You: dinner and a movie. Don't do just one, do both. If your palms feel sweaty when you get to the restaurant and you have to tell the host that you need a table for one, squeeze the book or sketchpad or knitting you have at your side, and remember the staff is more concerned about turning tables over efficiently than they are about your social status. Try to make eye contact with other diners. You're going to enjoy your meal as much as they are; there's no reason to hide.

At the movie, sit wherever you please, not where someone else likes it best. Laugh when the movie's funny, cry when it's tragic. Don't rush out at the end, staring at your feet. When you walk out, remember to think about having treated yourself to an evening with your own best company. You may not have enjoyed it like I do, and that's OK, but you will have done it. You don't need to do it again if you don't want to. But think about what the experience was like, and how it made you feel before, during, and after.

And think about whether this date relates to any feelings you might have that keep you from taking on a new project for fear of being odd.

BITING OFF MORE THAN I COULD CHEW

One day in the winter of 2004, I got an e-mail out of the blue from
an acquisitions editor at a major international publisher that was
planning to launch a new series of crafts books. She was looking for
an author for a crochet book, and she found my website (there still
weren't very many non-Geocities crochet websites back in '04). She
asked if I'd be interested in writing the book or if I knew someone
who might be.

Holy. Crap.

When I'd made the decision a few months earlier to work on my
crochet website full time, I was aware of the beginnings of the blog-
to-book phenomenon. Popular bloggers were getting book deals,
and I was not oblivious to it. I'd planned to work hard for at least a
year and then maybe figure out how to pitch a book. I did not think a
publisher would come to me. And I certainly didn't think a publisher
would come to me so soon. So very soon.

When this editor e-mailed me, I was twenty-seven years old. I had
not held a proper, full-time job in a few years. I was a grad-school
dropout two times over with a master's degree I didn't use. It would
be another couple of years before my work on the crochet website
would lead me to feel I was a proper, full-fledged, experienced editor.
And let's not forget that I'd barely been crocheting for a year, and
spent most of my crochet time editing patterns and not crocheting,

so the whole part about writing a how-to manual seemed ridiculous to me. Naturally, I was inclined to tell this editor that I was flattered but unqualified, and that I'd think hard about whether I knew of anyone who would be qualified and interested in writing her book.

But I hesitated. And in that moment of hesitation, I had a thought that changed everything.

The thought that changed everything was a flash-forward vision of sitting with my grandchildren and pulling a tattered, yellowed book off the shelf.

"Did you know, kids, that I wrote a book once?"

"No, Grandma, we didn't! Wow, you're swell."

Yup, this scene played out in dialogue worthy of *Leave It to Beaver*. It got me out of my downward spiral of naysaying and who-do-you-think-you-are-ing, that's for sure.

Oh hells yes, I wanted to write a book. Right here was an opportunity that landed right in my lap. It wouldn't be very adventurous to pass it up, now would it?

I asked the editor if they would consider a co-authorship.

She said they would.

I e-mailed a crochet designer I'd recently met and requested her phone number. Then I called her up and asked her to write a book with me.

Even writing this down right now, I can't believe I did that. I'm smirking and shaking my head at my own audacity.

It's one of my proudest moments.

Cecily Keim and I ended up writing two books together, and during those years of fevered working, I considered myself to be the technical writer and her to be the creative one. She gave me hell about that, and it's possible all this work about creativity that I do now is in part because she wouldn't put up with my BS about not being creative. I really did believe it at the time, though. I really did.

Sometimes, being creative is saying **YES**, then figuring out how to deal with the ramifications.

> Lauren Bacon wrote a stunning blog post about this perspective on decision-making: "The One Question You Must Ask (or, The World's Shortest Bucket List)." "When you're on your deathbed, what do you need to have experienced in order to feel you've lived a good and fulfilling life?" Read it at bit.ly/one-question.

FRUSTRATION AS MOTIVATION

If I could somehow avoid a space/time paradox and go back to one point in my life to whisper one sentence in my younger self's ear, and I really only had one sentence, I'd go back to some moment in later high school, when my younger self would be scowling with a red pen in her hand, scribbling carnage on the school newspaper. I'd whisper to her that it seems we have a knack for editing, and we might want to consider pursuing it professionally.

Alas, as an adolescent, I didn't have the self-awareness to find it obvious that the frustration—nay, *anger!*—I felt upon discovering typos in the news media might translate into a paycheck. Or that the decade it would take me to stumble onto that tidy answer would be fraught with doubt and confusion.

Have you experienced this sort of thing? Are there times when you're so baffled by how badly something is being done that you throw your hands in the air and just do it yourself, better? Do you get some kind of perverse satisfaction from that? From doing it better, from doing it right?

From my handy perspective in my late thirties, I see that my red-pen antics when I was younger fit very nicely into a pattern of motivation I've learned to rely on: I do great work when I'm intensely pissed off and know I can do better than whatever it is that's so irritating.

I launched a crochet website on a whim one weekend because I was sick of seeing blinking, poorly written Geocities sites with blurry flash photographs of poorly styled doilies. I didn't have crochet skills at the time, but I could make a website that wasn't purple and I could write a coherent sentence, so I did it. But I didn't just do it. I was irritated enough that I wrote a manifesto about the state of crochet online. Manifestos and irritation go hand in hand. Eventually, irritation turned into purpose, and that purpose fueled my projects for years.

Frustration can be a treasure trove of inspiration. Try to identify if there are annoyances in your life that you can flip around into opportunities for creative solutions. Even if the solution is only for yourself. At the very least, you'll remove one source of irritation from your life, and there's a chance you'll embark on an epic creative adventure.

TRY THIS!

MINE THE TRASH HEAP

BLOCK   PERFECTIONISM

When my husband and I were first dating, his brother was just starting grad school. He lived in a small apartment, and I'd been told of the unique ways he'd made that apartment his home, like by having a piece of foam custom cut to the odd, angled dimensions of his absurdly small bedroom. A bed won't fit properly? No problem.

Something else Eric, an economist, had done was create his own art. He bought some paintings from thrift stores and reused the canvases to knock off some of his favorite abstract artists. At the time, I was both baffled and awed by this—who would ever think to do something like that? What guts it took to use materials that way! Also, is that normal?

Looking back on this now, I wish I'd thought to do that when I was a poor, miserable grad student. Even now, most of the Mighty Ugly projects I do are with discarded materials and scraps—there's so much freedom to be found by seeing low-value objects as raw material.

Go to your recycling bin and pull out a couple handfuls of stuff—paper, containers, cardboard, doodads, whatever. Grab scissors, glue, paint, wire cutters, etc.

Set a timer for fifteen minutes. Make a structure of some sort—a gnome house, a bridge, a treehouse, whatever.

When you're done, keep it, or crush it and send it back to the bin.

FLIP IT AROUND: How would you make the same kind of thing out of more traditional craft materials of the sort you'd buy in a store? Would your construction process be the same or different? What about your assessment of the result? Does thinking about this incline you toward doing this exercise again? If it does, do it.

THE BOSS OF YOU

SELF-DOUBT   BLOCK

When I was first developing Mighty Ugly, I realized that I needed to be specific about the project. I couldn't just ask people to make something ugly. "Something" is way too general—people would have no idea what to do. So I ask people to make a creature. That provides a place to start, and as an added bonus, creatures provide high-test fuel for storytelling.

But most of the time, we don't have someone telling us what to make, we just feel compelled to make *something*. Like staring at a blank page when we want to write the great American novel, this is a horrible place to start.

To overcome the challenge of the blank page, try to find sources of direction. Join in when a bunch of friends decides to each work on a project of a similar sort, like learning how to cook Italian food or arrange flowers. Or phone up your local women's shelter to find out what kinds of donations they need, then knit that sort of thing for them.

Or embark on a less predictable adventure that's likely to provide lasting memories: ask a kid what to do.

When you have no idea how to even think of what to make, ASK FOR DIRECTIONS. Find a kid, preferably—one of your own or someone else's that you see relatively frequently, so they can hold you to your promise to make the thing—and ask them what they'd like you to make. Make no promise to them other than that you'll make it— don't tell them you'll make them the *perfect* thing, don't tell them you'll make them the *best* thing, don't even tell them you'll make them a *special* thing, and for the love of God, don't tell them what you'll make it out of, just in case your initial idea doesn't pan out. (And for the love of your sanity, don't accept a task to make any particular character from books, TV, or movies—about these things kids can be downright fanatical; best not to set yourself up to spark a tantrum from eyebrows the wrong shade of brown.)

Now, go make it. Kids have little concern for perfection, which is why they're the ones telling you what to do in this exercise and not your boss.

VARIATION: Rather than just naming a thing and making it, make the thing in the company of your pint-size pal. At various crossroads, or when you find yourself stuck, ask the kid what they want you to do— what color should the T-Rex's fingernails be? How big do you want the wheels of the Martian school bus? How many ruffles should the hedgehog princess's sleeves have?

FLIP IT AROUND: **Make it ugly. Do it with your small companion if you want. Compare and contrast their approach to making something ugly with yours.**

I DON'T KNOW

I have a tendency to feel immediate shame when I'm asked something and I don't know the answer. I don't know why I feel this way, but I always have. As if I should know absolutely everything, and any speck of ignorance is a failure. I've worked hard to accept how ridiculous that is, and one of the most successful strategies I've found is to think about times when people I really respect have copped to their own ignorance.

My eighth-grade science teacher, Mrs. Cappiello, had all sorts of awesome toys on her desk. Her desk was a ten-foot-long science table, so that's a lot of awesome toys. She taught us about things like electromagnetism and gravity. We were a bunch of newly adolescent pissants in a class involving lots of hands-on experimentation, and so every day we bombarded poor Mrs. Cappiello with an astonishing assortment of questions. From basic curiosities related to our assignments to truly outlandish hypotheticals involving time travel and alien life, we held nothing back.

What I remember most from that class is how frequently the expert in the room stood at the front of the class and said, "I don't know." At first I was a little shocked. The teacher didn't know *so much*. How did she even get this job? She didn't even use any more breath to tell us to look it up. She didn't say it with derision or frustration or eye-rolling. She was just all, "I don't know. Next question?"

So, it's OK not to know? Why isn't this a central part of every core curriculum? This woman's whole class was about tacitly teaching us how to find out answers for ourselves. I mean, she told us the answer when she knew it. She'd take a few minutes to look something up if the appropriate reference book was within reach. But mostly, she just admitted her ignorance and moved on.

And so, Mrs. Cappiello is one of my heroes. It's so very hard to stand in front of a group of people who look to you as an authority and admit to them that you don't know. Very hard. And it's even harder not to beat yourself up about the not knowing. The ugly voice starts to shout when this happens. **"NOW THEY KNOW YOU'RE A FAKE, YOU BIG FAKER!" "WHY DID YOU EVER THINK YOU WERE QUALIFIED TO STAND UP HERE IN FRONT OF THESE PEOPLE?" "THEY'RE ALL GOING TO HATE YOU NOW."**

When this happens to me, I think of Mrs. Cappiello. In her calm voice, she tells the ugly voice that she doesn't know. And then I tell the people I'm speaking with that I don't know. And then I move on, as if it's perfectly OK that I don't know.

Because it **IS PERFECTLY OK THAT I DON'T KNOW.**

FEATURETTE
On Confessing

Kate Bingaman-Burt is an illustrator and an assistant professor of graphic design at Portland State University who chronicled her daily purchases through drawings in a years-long project called Obsessive Consumption.* The initial incarnation of the project involved Kate drawing her credit-card statements and posting them online each month until she paid off her debt. That public grappling with something she felt ashamed of wasn't easy, but, pardon the pun, it paid off. Kate told me, "I had a few sleepless nights after I started sharing online. Revealing my debt was gut-twistingly awful and then committing to drawing all of my statements of shame every month just seemed horrifying at the time, but if I hadn't shared in that way, I know that I would still be dealing with my debt to this day."

Given her penchant for being so honest in public, it's no surprise that Kate brings her mistakes along with her successes into her classroom. "I am really open with my students about my own creative process, warts and all. I share with them good ideas and moves that

continued

continued

---

* She also illustrated this book! She is amazeballs!

I feel like I have made, along with some really crappy ones so they can learn from my stupid mistakes as well. I learn from them just as much as they learn from me, so being open and sharing the flaws helps all of us. I can talk through it and they can learn and laugh and hopefully not make those mistakes."

As an observer, I've always found Kate's confessionals to be a powerful reminder that I'm not alone in having habits I'm ashamed of. I feel stronger knowing that, and more comfortable talking about things I'd otherwise feel inclined to hide. Like when I don't know an answer I think I should know.

In 2012, Tess Vigeland left her job as host of NPR's Marketplace Money radio show, and she did it without having a new job lined up. The ensuing months were a roller coaster for her, from the highs of well-received freelance work to the lows of feeling convinced she'd never work again. Tess gave a refreshingly honest talk at the World Domination Summit in 2013 (a talk that led to a book deal). Being brutally honest about your fears and insecurities can be scary just with a friend, let alone in front of an audience of thousands. It's pretty much always worth it, though, because humans are awfully understanding in the face of naked honesty. Turn your phone off for half an hour and watch at bit.ly/tessvigeland.

TRY THIS!

TONE DEAF

FEAR OF FAILURE

SELF-DOUBT

PERFECTIONISM

One day, in the middle of a road trip, on a big driving day, we put in the Alanis Morissette CD, as you do. Staring out the window, we sang along to the whole thing. Ordinarily this would not be worthy of remark, but this forty-five minutes of singing was the first time I was ever aware that I was singing in tune.

My mother (hi, Mom) cannot sing in tune. Clinical tone deafness is a pretty specific diagnosis, but in our family the assertion has always been that Mom's tone deaf; whether she technically is or not is beside the point.

Growing up, I was put into this category too. Aside from a year playing violin when I was nine and a year very awkwardly singing in the fifth-grade choir, music was not a part of my life.

Music continues to confuse me. I don't think I've ever sung "Happy Birthday" in tune. Especially when I was a kid, things that confused me made me uncomfortable. I didn't know how to ask about things I felt I should know. Other people seemed to just *get* music, and I just didn't.

I wish that someone had pointed out that my occasionally uncanny ability to imitate other people's speech is incontrovertible evidence that I'm not, in fact, tone deaf. But whatever.

So that road trip. An entire Alanis Morissette CD sung in tune. I was imitating her voice. In mimicking her, I nailed it. When the songs were over, I was baffled and amazed. To be honest, my self-concept still hasn't adjusted to this I'm-not-tone-deaf development.

I'm still not very comfortable singing in public, but I do sing a heckuva lot more than I used to, especially in private.

I know I promised we wouldn't do too much more introspection, but I didn't say we'd do *none*. This exercise shouldn't be of the painful variety.

⇩ ⇩ ⇩

Take a few minutes alone with yourself, and think about whether there's something you feel painfully self-conscious about. Or, more likely, think of all the things you feel self-conscious about. What's the root of that self-consciousness? Were you, like me, told when you were little that you couldn't do it? Did someone once make a snide remark? Or is it something more subtle, that no one has commented on but you?

On the next page, write them down in the appropriate column—have you been told by someone else that you're no good at it, or have you told yourself you're no good at it (or, if it's both, can you remember who told you first?)?

Now, challenge yourself to DO those things. Not in any big way with fanfare and cake. Just see if you can actually do it, or how it feels to try. Take a drive and sing your heart out, or just close your door and quietly put pen to paper. What does it feel like to do this? Awkward and painful? Defiant? Fun? Consider whether you'd like to start disbelieving the assertion that you *can't* do it.

SOMEONE TOLD ME
I CAN'T DO THIS

I TELL MYSELF
I CAN'T DO THIS

TRY THIS!

COMMENCEMENT ADDRESS-A-THON

FEAR OF FAILURE

SELF-DOUBT

PERFECTIONISM

Do you ever sit around, thinking about your future and pondering the wise words of the commencement speaker at your high school or college graduation?

Yeah, neither do I. I don't even remember who delivered the wise words at my college graduation. I remember what I wore (cut-off shorts and a T-shirt under my polyester gown), and I remember what I did afterwards (have lunch with my roommates and our families), but the speech that was intended to send me into the welcoming arms of adulthood? Not a thing. Just like I rolled my eyes to survey my angst whenever someone told me I should savor my youthful days as the best time of my life, sage advice was lost on me. I bet it was lost on you too.

But now there's this thing called YouTube, and on this YouTube are countless video recordings of speeches by people far wiser, far more accomplished, and far more famous than whoever the speaker was at my college graduation. And at this point in my life, I'm more than open to hearing what they have to say.

So I watch commencement addresses. I watch *a lot* of commencement addresses. Free and easy access to commencement addresses is what makes me marvel at the wonder of the internet.

One of my favorites is the speech Conan O'Brien delivered to the Dartmouth class of 2011, during which he waxed honestly and profoundly about his fall from *The Tonight Show*. "Your path at twenty-two will not necessarily be your path at thirty-two or forty-two. One's dream is constantly evolving, rising and falling, changing course." Indeed, Conan, indeed.*

He also said something that's at the heart of Mighty Ugly: "It's not easy, but if you accept your misfortune and handle it right, your perceived failure can become a catalyst for profound reinvention." Who knows from reinvention when they're eighteen or twenty-two? I'd put money on *zero people*.

At his address to the University of the Arts class of 2012, author Neil Gaiman highlighted one of the most valuable lessons I've ever learned: that people often achieve brilliance when they simply don't know any better. "People who know what they're doing know the rules, and they know what is possible and what is impossible . . . If you don't know it's impossible, it's easier to do."

---

* Dear Conan,
If I throw myself a fortieth birthday party, would you come give a commencement address to my friends and me? As we embark upon middle age, I think we'll be open to some wise words and laughs. I'll make a cake, or whatever.
Cheers,
Kim

I could go on, but that would defeat the purpose of this exercise.

Which is, as you've likely surmised, to go on a commencement-address bender. Fire up your YouTube and spend a few hours pretending that people you admire are speaking directly to you. To boot, you can pretend you attended one of the schmancy universities that bring in the most famous of people with smart words to share.

Here's a list of some of my favorite commencement addresses to get you started (go to YouTube and search for "First-Name Last-Name commencement YEAR"). And don't be shy about clicking on the videos YouTube suggests at the end of each clip; I've found some gems just surfing around.

* Conan O'Brien, Dartmouth College, 2011
* Neil Gaiman, University of the Arts, 2012
* J.K. Rowling, Harvard University, 2008
* Joss Whedon, Wesleyan, 2013
* Jacqueline Novogratz, Gettysburg College, 2012
* Steve Jobs, Stanford University, 2005
* Lisa Kudrow, Vassar College, 2010

FLIP IT AROUND: Picture yourself at twenty-one. Write that youngster a commencement address. Include any kind of truth nugget you know now that you wish you'd known then. Avoid feeling pressure to write pithy sound bites. (If you're twenty-one-ish or younger, picture me, the thirty-something blowhard deigning to give you advice, and give me some advice of your own. Or if you're not feeling so powerful right now, jot down some things you think I'd tell you. Keep in mind that I'd almost certainly say these things to you in earnest and not with my sarcastic voice.)

Neil Gaiman's "Make Good Art" commencement address has been made into a wee hardcover book, illustrated by Chip Kidd. You know, in case you want to carry a copy around with you at all times. Not that I know what that's like.

TURN IT OFF

There's the old adage that love finds you when you're not looking for it. I think the same is true for inspiration. We can't force our neurons to fire off new ideas. All we can do is trust that the ideas will come, and feed our brains the kinds of ingredients that tend to allow that to happen. Each of us enjoys a different recipe, and I urge you to pay attention to what gets your neurons firing.

I seesaw between consuming an exceptional amount of media—current events, science news, pop culture reports, novels, blogs, crafts books, commentary, television, radio—and turning it all off.

I make stuff in both states. When I've got my maw open to the fire hose, I pick out a steady stream of things that spark reactions I want to write about and projects I want to do. And I often end up bouncing different elements off each other in very satisfying ways that lead to new lines of thinking and new ideas for stuff to make.

When I turn away from the fire hose, I do far more from-the-insides-of-me creating. This is when I'm more inclined to write out directions than follow them. It's when I work on large-scale projects that require a lot of energy and the kind of focus I can't achieve when I'm assaulting myself with information.

I can't do the quiet work without having fueled up on the fire hose, and I can't endure the fire hose without taking serious breaks.

"If you're true to yourself, then what you have to share is universal."

—CHRISTOPHER DOYLE, CINEMATOGRAPHER

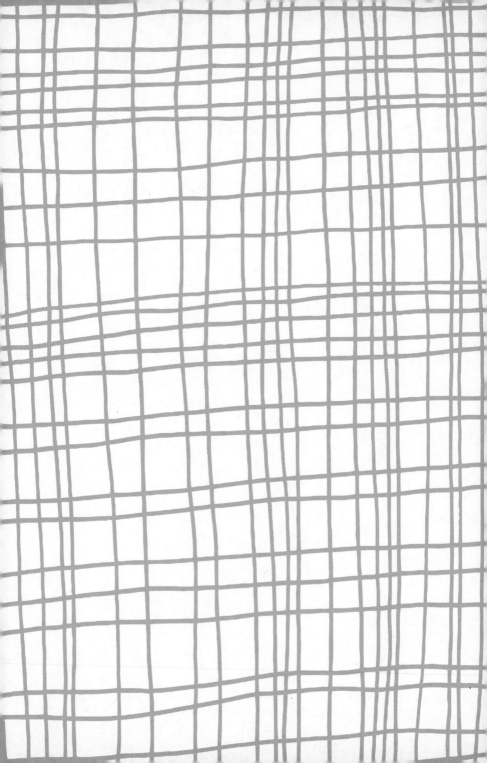

SO, YOU'VE BEEN GETTING IN TOUCH with your creative drive, and you've been making stuff. Most excellent!

The rest of the book is about establishing a rhythm so you can start to rely on your creative practice as a normal, and important, part of your life. We'll find you some time to set aside so you don't constantly feel like you're too busy to make stuff, we'll think about how you might start to share your creations with others, we'll address the inevitable challenges you'll face, and we'll start to look ahead to where all this creativity might take you down the road.

This chapter, to a great extent, is about rules. Not the kind you'll automatically want to rebel against (or is it just me who has that immediate reaction to rules?), but the kind that will help you explore and establish your creative practice. A wide-open expanse can be oh-so-very intimidating; rules help us break that expanse down into more easily navigable areas.

Some rules will be broad and simple, like, "Just start saying you make pottery or software." Some will be very narrow and specific, like to perform the same task at the same time every day for a certain number of days. The idea is to make it easy to get creative—all you'll have to do is follow the rules.

Let's get to it.

Imagine my delight when I discovered that Kate Bingaman-Burt (see page 107), delivered a brilliant TEDxPortland talk about rules. "My projects all rely on a system of rules to give order to the initial chaos of ideas. Rules help me structure my workflow. They keep me making and they keep me moving . . . Rules are good. Constraint yields creation."

Watch her whole talk at bit.ly/katebb-tedx.

SECTION 1: ESTABLISH A REGULAR PRACTICE

TRY THIS!

THREE LITTLE PICTURES

PROCRASTINATION   BLOCK   PERFECTIONISM

I'm interested in almost everything. You'd think this would be a good thing, and it is, if you're a kid. When you're a kid, you can feel giddy in the face of the world being open to you in its entirety. As I grew up and started coming up against having to choose what to be *most* interested in, though, I started to feel plagued. If I enjoyed all my classes in school except for whichever ones were taught by teachers I didn't like, how was I supposed to choose just one subject to focus on in college? After I eventually managed to choose a major in college, I ended up spending most of my time in graduate school suffocating under the crushing weight of all the paths I hadn't chosen.

Whether you're inclined, like me, to be a jack-of-all-trades—I try to own the derogatory *dilettante*—or have known since you were six that there's only one thing you want to be when you grow up, certainly we can all see the value in having at least some constraints that limit the scope of possibility. Not constraints like draconian regulations and denials of flexibility, but constraints that allow us to narrow our focus enough to see infinite potential in a more manageable set of possibilities. Constraints can set creativity free.

I thrive on working to a deadline. Deadlines keep my imagination in check; I can't pursue every possible angle if I need to have a coherent piece finished in a week. Deadlines also prevent me from being a perfectionist, even though I'm not usually inclined toward perfectionism. I am, however, inclined to do my best possible work, and I'm well aware that I'm my own worst critic. A deadline forces me to do my best work and then send it off, preventing me from further fiddling or changing course after yet one more early-morning eureka moment.

Constraints force us to focus when we might otherwise be inclined to drift. They limit our resources so we have to apply our ingenuity to achieve our goal. They enable us to let go.

⇓ ⇓ ⇓

Grab a small camera and keep it with you at all times for a week (your phone camera will do just fine if you don't want to lug around another device; if you're camera-shy,* feel free to carry a pencil and paper and sketch what you see). **EACH DAY OF THE WEEK, TAKE THREE PICTURES ACCORDING TO THE CONSTRAINTS LISTED ON THE FOLLOWING PAGE.** It doesn't matter when you take them, if you take them all at

---

* See what I did there?

once or if you spread them throughout the day. You don't need to make art, just take some snapshots (or make some sketches). The goal here is to focus on just doing it, not so much on what the images look like at the end of the week (though having those images may be a wonderful bonus).

DAY ONE: Just take three photos by the end of the day.
DAY TWO: Take three photos of red things.
DAY THREE: Take three photos of living things.
DAY FOUR: Take three photos of moving things.
DAY FIVE: Take three photos of yourself.
DAY SIX: Take three photos of surprises.
DAY SEVEN: Just take three photos by the end of the day.

Now, what was each day like? Were some days easier than others? How did the first and last days, without constraints, compare to the middle days? Did your feelings about taking the photos or sketching the pictures change over the course of the week? Did the quality or tone of your images evolve? Are you left with any thoughts about how you might apply constraints to boost your enjoyment of everyday things?

FLIP IT AROUND: Do this again, but make the pictures ugly.

> "The things that inspire me most are things I experience firsthand in my own life. My relationships. Fabrics I see on the street. Patterns. Colors. Other people I personally know who are successfully creating their own brand of art. My inspiration is rarely abstract; it comes from actual things I touch, see, and feel."
>
> —JASIKA NICOLE, ACTOR AND ARTIST

TRY THIS!

DAILY PROJECT

FEAR OF FAILURE   SELF-DOUBT   PERFECTIONISM

PROCRASTINATION   BLOCK

The first daily project I became aware of was in the mid-2000s when lots of knit-bloggers participated in a 365-photo challenge. The idea was to take a self-portrait every day for a year, and many people were sharing their daily selfies on their blog or on Flickr. I started a few times myself, but rarely got further than a month into it. But I loved watching people's progress in the days long before Instagram and Twitter.

Since then, I've watched countless kinds of daily projects progress, from a single person's feat, like artist Noah Scalin's Skull-a-Day project and Kate Bingaman-Burt's Obsessive Consumption drawings, to projects attracting lots of people to participate, like the thirty-day drawing challenge Jasika Nicole took on and chronicled on her blog, involving specific tasks or quests for each day. And of course there was the now-famous *Julie and Julia,* for which blogger Julie Powell committed to cook every recipe in Julia Child's classic *Mastering the Art of French Cooking.*

> "I posted every single image [for a thirty-day drawing challenge], no matter my own personal feelings about it. It was important for me to recognize and not be embarrassed about the fact that my art is a process—normally I only post projects that I am very proud of, but not everything I make is incredible, and there is no shame in that."
>
> —JASIKA NICOLE, ACTOR AND ARTIST

A daily challenge is enticing, because the big deal about it—to commit to making or doing a well-defined thing every day—is mitigated by the baby steps involved. When each day you do just the one thing, eventually you end up with an impressive collection of creations.

Commit to a daily project. I won't presume to dictate the sort of project you should do or for how long you should do it. I've learned, for example, that I need a *reason* to make such a big commitment. Just taking a photo of myself every day doesn't resonate with any particular need I have, and neither does the arbitrary commitment to do it for a whole year. So as you choose the kind of adventure to take, be honest with yourself about what you want to accomplish, how short is too short, and how long is too long.

Do you want to improve upon or learn a new skill? Amass a collection of art or crafts you made? Prove to yourself that you can follow through? Find something to blog about?

Can you accomplish your goal in a week? A month? A year?

Will you get bored in a year? Will you be able to find your groove in only a week?

VARIATION: Take a step back from the *daily* part and challenge yourself to complete X number of things in Y amount of time, like how artist Sonya Philip made one hundred dresses in a year (we'll learn more about her project later in the book).

Here are some ideas to consider:

* Make a doodle a day. (Variation: Make a cat doodle a day, or a dog doodle, or a space-creature doodle.)
* Bake a new muffin recipe every week for three months.
* Be very broad like my friend Miriam Felton, and embark upon a year of making—chronicling something you've made by hand every day, from cooking to gardening to knitting and sewing.
* Take a photo of a particular thing every day—your packed lunch, a bicycle on the street, a dust bunny . . .
* Photograph, paint, draw, or sculpt a self-portrait every day.
* Commit an act of charity every day.
* Read and review X number of books in a year.
* Craft for fifteen minutes a day, cataloging what you do in a journal or blog.
* Make all of your kid's clothes for a year.
* FLIP IT AROUND: Whatever you choose to do, make it ugly. Or make every X item ugly—like, take a self-portrait photo every day but once a week make an ugly face. See Ugly Face Wednesdays for inspiration at bit.ly/ugly-face-wed.

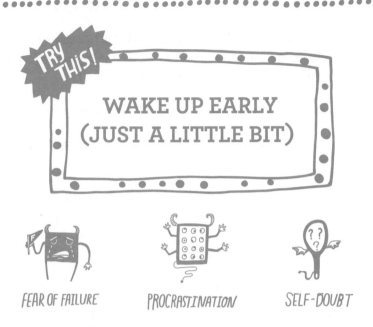

TRY THIS!

WAKE UP EARLY (JUST A LITTLE BIT)

FEAR OF FAILURE　　*PROCRASTINATION*　　*SELF-DOUBT*

TIME. Yowza.

How often do we deny ourselves pursuit of our own interests because we insist we don't have the time?

Think about this. Have you wanted to start doing something on a regular basis but given yourself the excuse that you don't have time? No time to read more books, no time to take a ceramics class, no time to learn how to knit, no time to take tennis lessons.

This very thing is a huge barrier to entry for anything new we want to learn, isn't it? **TIME.** When we already know how to do something, it's just not as much of a burden on our time. When we know how to bake a great cake, we wake up the morning of the party and we bake the cake. No big deal, we barely think about it.

But when we want to learn something new, and in this stage of battling demons when we're really just itching make this great amazing change in our life and have it be done with already, the time factor is downright daunting.

So here's what I propose.

Wake up fifteen minutes early every day for three weeks. (Do it every day so your body adjusts to the minor shift and you're not yo-yoing your sleep patterns into disarray.) With those fifteen minutes, scratch your creative itch. If you suffer the same plague I did, which is not knowing exactly what you even want to do, here are some suggestions. Note that I'm suggesting them not because I think any one in particular will be the light that turns on in your soul, but in the way my grandmother used to insist I try on every dress in my size, "just to see the style."

* Doodle (check out Zentangle if you want a guided approach to doodling).
* Learn (or remind yourself how) to knit, crochet, cross-stitch, or embroider using books or YouTube.
* Play. If you won't wake anyone else up, pull out your recorder from middle school (what? You don't have one at the bottom of your closet?) and start with "Mary Had a Little Lamb."
* Cook or bake something.
* Write.
* Go out and take some photographs or sketch your favorite neighborhood vista.

This exercise is specifically about waking up early and not about setting aside fifteen minutes at some other part of the day, because it's *hard* to set aside fifteen minutes every day. Knocking off your fifteen minutes before you even shower or have coffee or eat breakfast means you're starting off your day having done something to feed your creativity. So you can go through your day knowing you've done it, and feeling the feelings that go along with that, whatever those feelings might be. Hopefully, after a few days or weeks, those feelings will be related in some way to pride or contentment or inspiration.

VARIATION: Take a class. Part with your money and commit. Unless you live in a very, very small town (in which case I'd bet money a neighbor would be willing to teach you something they know), you have options. Maybe a community center, lifelong-learning program, local college, the school board—one or all of these organizations should offer classes of all sorts, from arts and crafts to music to foreign languages to poetry or creative writing. Find one that will help you scratch your itch, sign up, and then, most importantly, show up. (No promises that you'll *enjoy* the class. If you don't, try a different one next time.)

In 2013, Portland, Oregon, fashion designer Kirsten Moore started posting Instagram photos of birds she'd drawn in her day planner, one bird each day. I knew Kirsten and didn't know she was an artist, and I was enthralled by her daily birds. Six months into her project, she wrote a blog post explaining that she'd decided at the new year to improve her drawing skills, and had committed to drawing a bird in her calendar every day. It's amazing to see her first, rough attempts alongside her breathtaking later ones. At the time I write this, she's still drawing birds, and she started drawing bonus birds on separate paper that she sells. She also started collaborating with a painter on some pieces. See if she's still at it at bit.ly/kirsten-moore.

If you're battling demons of doubt and intimidation, you might draw some inspiration from Kirsten's desire simply to get better at something. Her goal wasn't to draw an extraordinary thing every day—it was to work on her skills. Take that, demons.

FEATURETTE

Exercises in Commitment

Artist Sonya Philip challenged herself to sew one hundred dresses in a year. "When I was growing up, and even through my college years," she says, "I had this idea of creative and artistic people. I thought that it was all about waiting for inspiration to strike—sitting in a garret or whatnot, eyes upturned. It was a very romanticized notion. For 100 Acts of Sewing, I kid you not, I have spreadsheets and monthly goals. This is completely contrary to my thinking of creativity as something spontaneous. It becomes about diligence, repetition, routine, all those decidedly unsexy things."

continued

Committing to a long-term project can be romantic and exciting, but it's the unexpected hurdles along the way that make it so transformative. Kirsty Hall made art in a Mason jar every day for a year, and placed the jars in public places with instructions for how to alert her that they were found. "When I started it, it didn't feel like a creative risk, but in retrospect, it was massive. Giving my art away daily for a year, stepping outside the gallery system, and letting go of control of my work were all huge risks, and it was a deep learning experience for me. It was wonderful but often difficult. I could have quit at any time, but I'm stubborn and wanted to see it through to the end."

Indeed, simply knowing you can keep at it through such a long commitment can be valuable. "I don't think I've felt truly stuck in a big way since I did my Skull-A-Day project," says artist and author Noah Scalin. "Once I turned the taps on full blast they just kept flowing."

The pride and sustained inspiration that can come from seeing it through is something almost everyone mentions when I ask them about their experience with a daily project. It's as if simply following through with the commitment is as important as —or possibly more important than—the individual acts of making art or crafts or writing or music.

Something to keep in mind as you decide on a way to challenge yourself, eh?

Artist Phil Hansen made so much pointillist art in school that he developed a permanent tremor in his hand. Rather than give up art, he decided to embrace the shake. "Learning to be creative within the confines of our limitations is the best hope we have to transform ourselves, and, collectively, transform our world." Watch his TED talk and prepare to be overcome with hope at bit.ly/phil-hansen-TED.

HABIT

There's a whole micro-industry out there that compiles things famous people have said about their creative practice. A few minutes on Google will point you to books, interviews, and articles containing more information and sound bites than would be wise to consume in one go. Many of these works involve endorsement of routines and rituals. Bear in mind, of course, that what works for one person is sure to drive another mad, so read up on famous people's habits while remembering that whiskey and a pack of cigarettes at seven every morning may not actually be the best path to take.

Forming a creative habit is what this chapter is all about, and I've found it's the little things that make creative habits stick. Dramatic resolutions to make stuff or write novels or run a marathon make for dramatic disappointments in the frequent case that you don't follow through all the way to the dramatic end.

No, it's the small steps that add up to grand creative achievement. It's taking a big idea and making it happen over time in tiny increments. And habit—whether loosely structured or fully regimented—is what enables us to do it.

For me, well, I require an alarming amount of *lack of structure*. Even a little bit of the wrong kind of structure makes me feel, and behave, like a caged animal. So my creative habit is simple, always. I rarely set myself more than one goal to achieve each day, and I don't care how I get there. If I do it first thing in the morning, great. If I can't quite manage to get it together till right before I go to bed, fine. Whatever happens the rest of the day is not a waste of time, it's the stuff that keeps my ideas flowing and my productivity moving forward at an acceptable clip.

When I really dig down deep into a project, I wear headphones and a cape to get into the right mindset. The headphones are real, though I don't always plug them in—it's the feeling of tuning out that they enable that's important to me. The cape is figurative; it's a thing that reminds me that I'm capable of doing whatever it is I'm setting out to do. Like the proverbial string tied around a finger, I often wear a ring as my cape.*

With ring on finger and headphones on ears, I'm transformed into the writing machine I know I am (or the stitching machine, or the sewing machine [not literally]). It's not that I feel like I can't write without them; it's that I immediately feel like I know I can when I do.

I've spoken with people who always listen to the same music when they get creative, or who make stuff only at night or only in the morning, or who only write at a particular coffee shop with a particular hot beverage in hand. The idea is to find a trigger that helps you snap into creative mode, and to poke around until you figure out how to fit it into a habit you enjoy. In other words, don't force yourself into a routine you don't enjoy and that doesn't actually fuel your creativity.

> Books about habit abound; spend some time at the library flipping around until you find one that strikes a chord. My favorite is choreographer Twyla Tharp's *The Creative Habit*. She draws on decades of prolific creativity to encourage all readers to lay a foundation for sustained practice. From a less anecdotal angle, Charles Duhigg's journalistic account of the science behind habit, *The Power of Habit*, comes highly recommended.

---

* Betsy Cross (read more about her on page 39) made the ring. I'm not lying when I say I'm her biggest fan.

SOW THE SEEDS OF HABIT

PROCRASTINATION

BLOCK

When I want to establish a new kind of routine from scratch (I'd be lying if I implied a habit is forever—I often play with what works, as circumstances always seem to be changing around me, and my own desires shift over time), I find it useful to do a little research before I start to just shoot around in the dark. On the following couple of pages, you'll find graphs to fill in to help you discover when you're most likely to feel like making stuff, so you can start to take steps to establish a creative habit around those times.

What's important here is to keep track of what you *want* to be doing, rather than what you actually do (and don't even go to what you think you *should* be doing). That'll perhaps make more sense when you take a look at the graphs.

OVER THE COURSE OF A DAY—USE A DIFFERENT-COLORED PEN TO CHART EACH DAY OF A WEEK ON THE SAME GRAPHS—MARK DOWN HOW INSPIRED TO CREATE YOU FEEL, AND HOW DRAINED YOU FEEL. At the time of day indicated on the x-axis of each graph, put a dot on a scale of one to ten. At the end of the week, you'll probably see some clear trends. Use this information to see if you can rearrange your expectations for your day to allow for some time to make stuff when you're feeling most creative.

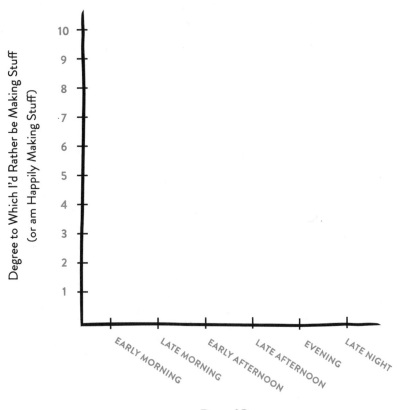

Time of Day

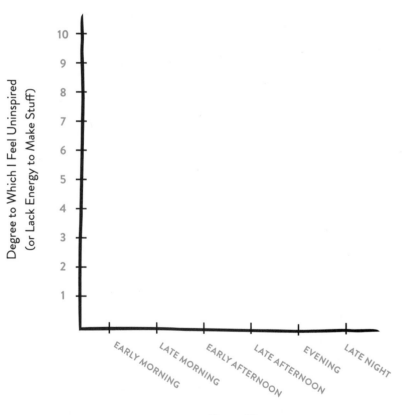

Degree to Which I Feel Uninspired (or Lack Energy to Make Stuff)

10
9
8
7
6
5
4
3
2
1

EARLY MORNING   LATE MORNING   EARLY AFTERNOON   LATE AFTERNOON   EVENING   LATE NIGHT

Time of Day

On Making Time

If it turns out that your optimal creative time is when you have to be doing something else like, you know, your job, see if you can find a creative solution. Can you make stuff on your lunch hour? Shift your work hours by an hour? Of course, it may end up that you have to train yourself to make do with what you have. Rachael Herron, who writes novels in addition to working more than fifty hours a week as an emergency dispatcher, made a Herculean effort to do just that: "In 2008, I made myself a promise I would write every day. I would put it first, even if it meant getting up at 4:00 a.m. (which, for several years, it did). My writing was the most important thing in my life besides family, and I suddenly wondered why, then, it was the last thing I got around to doing. I discovered that if I got my real work done in the morning before my job, my brain was relaxed for the rest of the day. I'd done the important thing! The rest of the day could fall apart, and I could still call myself a writer for that day."

Something I work hard at is showing up during my set-aside creative time even when I'm inclined not to—maybe I'm tired, or feeling down, or I'm questioning my ability to do this thing, or something that seems more important is tugging at my attention. Rachael subscribes to an approach I tend to preach, and I appreciate that she reminds me that "one of the most important parts of being an artist is working through the absolute suckitude—showing up and doing it anyway, even though we're 100 percent convinced we're terrible at it."

Rachael says that when she looks back at a novel, she can't tell the difference between parts she wrote when she was pushing through that suckitude and parts she wrote when she was feeling totally in the zone. Me? Not so much. I can always tell when I forced myself to fill a page with words. But even when I notice that I wrote something crappy when I was feeling crappy, I'm always happy to spend the time and effort to revise it—and I'd much rather work on making something better than not have anything on the page at all.

WHEN AN APPLE IS A PAINTBRUSH

The fall my son was two and a half, we declared one unexpectedly sunny Tuesday to be Apple Day. We'd go apple picking in the morning, then spend the afternoon making apple crumble and doing apple crafts.

Naturally, the plan was more, shall we say, *idyllic* than the reality. For example, the plan didn't involve me driving over a parking divider at the orchard, or us getting home so late that we wouldn't have enough time to do any cooking at all.

But the crafts would be quick and simple, and I was excited. The idea was to hack a couple of apples in half so my son could use them like stamps. I'd forgotten that I didn't have any general-use paint in the house, so I watered down some very thick finger paints and put some red, yellow, and green paint into bowls. I hastily cut out a tree shape from scrap paper and pasted it to a page. All was set for him to paint an apple tree with apples he'd picked.

I showed him what I had in mind, and he dunked the first apple into the watery paint with a big smile on his face. He planted it down on the paper, picked it up, and seemed pleased with the apple shape that resulted. Then he put the apple right back down on that spot, and smeared the paint all over the page. Now his smile was enormous, and he spent the next half hour using apples as if they were palm-size paint brushes.

My initial inclination to say, "No, wait! This is apple *stamping*, not painting!" was swallowed in a gulp, and I ended up enjoying watching his face while he did his thing. He was absorbed and happy, and so very proud of his paintings.

Kids are a constant reminder that the best-laid plan is often an exercise in futility. However frustrating it might be when we need them to go along with our adult schemes like grocery shopping and doing the dishes, much of the time what we need to do for them is let go of our expectations and follow their leads.

It's a lesson we'd do well to remember in our own adult pursuits. Sometimes an apple is an apple. Sometimes it's a stamp, and sometimes it's a smearer of paint. It's up to us to let go of our fantasies and experiment in reality until we, too, find ourselves absorbed and happy.

FILL IN THE . . .

FEAR OF FAILURE

SELF-DOUBT

PERFECTIONISM

PROCRASTINATION

BLOCK

Here's a more qualitative approach to establishing a creative habit. Rather than quantifying your feelings in numbers, we'll take a look at how your mood shifts throughout the day.

Do you remember fill-in-the-blank stationery from when you were a kid? Fashioned after office receptionists' note pads with sections for who called, at what time, and what the call was about, these pages let kids write a "letter" home in about fifteen seconds.

> Dear **MOM AND DAD**,
>
> I'm having a **BLAST** at summer camp. My favorite sport is **KICKBALL**. The weather has been **DREARY**, and the food is **EDIBLE**. Please send **CANDY**.
>
> Love,
> **KIM**

We're going to write ourselves some letters like these in an effort to gauge how our moods shift over the course of a day, so we can set ourselves up to shift our habits successfully, rather than try things out at random.

We all know our moods color our experiences of, well, pretty much everything. When I'm feeling stuck or overwhelmed or stressed, I respond very differently to both positive and negative stimuli than I do when I'm feeling rested and balanced and productive. So to maintain a semblance of balanced perspective, I try to consider some basic questions under different circumstances and see if my answers vary. Sometimes it's a waste of time and sometimes I feel like a damn genius, providing myself with brilliant insight into my own mind. Either way, I end up satisfied—for getting to roll my eyes at myself or for starting to move past whatever's dragging me down. And this can be especially helpful if you're trying to figure out when to make time for making stuff.

Admittedly, doing this as a mental exercise isn't always the most reliable or efficient task, so for you, dear reader, I've put the exercise down in words. I'm going use it too.

MAKE FIVE COPIES OF THE FOLLOWING PARAGRAPH, AND PLACE EACH ONE WHERE YOU'LL BE SURE TO SEE IT AT THE TIMES LISTED (obviously, adjust the times and situations to match your actual day). Then fill them out at those times. Don't think; just fill in the blanks. Don't consider what you wrote the last time; just write what comes to mind right now. The next day, look back over your answers. Does anything jump out at you? If you were grumpy, are you usually grumpy at that time of day? If you were utterly consistent, does that tell you anything useful that you can apply to your creative practice?

Date: _____ Time: _____

When I look up, I see _____, and I want to _____.
NOUN   VERB

My feet feel _____. I hear something that sounds like
ADJECTIVE

_____, and I want to _____. My job is making me
NOUN   VERB

_____. This weekend, I will _____. Oh man, I just
ADJECTIVE OR VERB   VERB

_____ chicken pot pie. When I close my eyes, just for a
VERB

moment, I see _____. In a perfect world, I'd turn on the radio
NOUN

right now and hear _____. I sure wish I could _____
NOUN   VERB

right now. Well, self, until next time, I have this one word for you:

_____.
ANYTHING

Fill in the blanks at varying times throughout your day. For example: first thing upon waking up in the morning, right when you arrive at your desk at work, during your lunch, right when you get home from work, immediately before you go to sleep.

What kinds of trends do you see? Are you most alert and optimistic at a certain time of day? Do you feel grumpy when you get home from work? Do these trends correspond in any useful way with the graphs you completed in the previous exercise? Think about how you can use all of this information together to carve out time for creative activities.

TAKE STOCK

SELF-DOUBT   BLOCK

It's time to examine our surroundings. You've done the work of smoking out your internal demons so you can fight them fairly; now it's time to apply the same sort of approach to the physical world. Perhaps that's not the best metaphor; we're not actually going to fight a war in the physical world. Anyway, you'll see what I mean.

Our surroundings can significantly affect our mood, and our mood can significantly affect our experience. You're spending a lot of energy working on your creative experience—it's time to apply some of that energy to the place where you do your creating. This could be at work, but I'm going to assume it's at home somewhere.

Does your ugly voice tell you that you can't invite people over because your home is a mess, or uninteresting, or uncomfortable, or, worst of all, that you're a terrible host so don't even bother? One corner of your house at a time, we're going to tell that voice to sit down.

One of the first things I do when I'm feeling twitchy is to rearrange a room. I started doing this when I was a teenager. I'd wake up one morning completely unable to live in my skin for one more second, so I'd tie a bandana around my head and spend the day cleaning up and moving all my furniture around. One of my favorite feelings is waking up the next morning in a fresh place. Now, just the thought of that kind of change might give you hives. That's OK. You don't have to be so all-or-nothing about it, but sprucing up your creative space will help you feel, and simply *be*, more creative.

Identify the place in your home where you spend more of your creative time than anywhere else. Could be the kitchen table, or maybe you have a craft room. If you're a knitter, crocheter, embroiderer, or hand-sewer, maybe it's the comfy chair in front of the television. If you're a painter, maybe it's the nook by the window. Turn all the lights on, make a thorough examination of this space, and catalog all the items in it and within view of it: lamps, knickknacks, photo graphs, furniture, appliances, art, window dressings, etc. Make a list on the next page. Put an asterisk next to the items you love, an "X" next to the items you hate, and an arrow next to the items you hate that you have to keep because your partner or roommate loves them. Refer to the list in the next exercise.

CATALOG OF ITEMS

HAPPY LITTLE VIGNETTES

FEAR OF FAILURE

SELF-DOUBT

PERFECTIONISM

PROCRASTINATION

BLOCK

A few years ago we removed most of one wall of our living room. We put in French doors so we could still have the option of closing it off if we wanted to, and the renovation left us with about two feet of wall space between the French doors and the entranceway from the front door of the house. After lots of hours looking for ideas online, I decided what we needed to do was make a small table where we could keep our keys and bus passes and spare change. My husband had the idea of using an old door from our ninety-year-old house, and he fashioned the table—which is like a box turned sideways so you can put stuff inside it like a shelf—from that and some scrap wood he had laying around. With the table in place, I hung a key rack on the wall above it, and above that, a ceramic owl plate his great-aunt made in the '70s. I put some books and an old camera inside the box part of the table, and on top I set a clay bowl our neighbor's kid made.

I love this tiny part of our home. It's one of the first things I see when I enter my house, and I feel content every time. Thinking about my home as a collection of small areas makes it far less daunting when it comes to decorating. I'm no interior designer, but I know what I like and my husband knows what he likes, and by keeping our focus narrow, we're able to assemble our things in a way that makes us both happy.

This is why we're paying so much attention to the place where you spend your creative time. You should not only love this space, it should inspire you. **SO WITH YOUR LIST FROM THE PREVIOUS EXERCISE IN HAND, DO THE FOLLOWING:**

⇩ ⇩ ⇩

Start in one corner of the room or nook you chose for the last exercise, and create what decor people call a "vignette"—a small area that's perfectly put together, from furniture to doodads to stuff on the wall.

The goal here is to create at least this one space in your home that you love with abandon. Move furniture around, hang (different) prints or photos or art. Insert or remove some knickknacks. Avoid the stuff you marked as hated; highlight the stuff you marked as loved.

Work with what you have, and steal things from other rooms if you want to. The idea here is not to acquire new stuff, but to use the stuff you already have in ways that make you happier. When you sit down to make something, your gaze should wander onto things that fuel your motivation to create.

If this exercise made you smile a very big smile, try doing it with other corners of your home or office too. I certainly applied what I learned from my entranceway vignette when I designed my studio space (which is also our guest room).

FLIP IT AROUND: Can you salvage something from your list that you hate? Can paint or Mod Podge or refinishing or reframing transform it into something likable? If it's something you're stuck with because someone you live with loves it, would they be open to altering it in some way that will endear it to you too? And are there concessions you can make in return?

SECTION 2: SHOW & TELL

TRY THIS!

SHOW (AND TELL)

FEAR OF FAILURE   SELF-DOUBT   PERFECTIONISM

IF YOU HAVEN'T ALREADY, TELL SOMEONE OR SOME PEOPLE ABOUT WHAT YOU MAKE. Yes, you may feel nervous about this. Do it anyway.

This is scary. You may fear that you'll end up feeling ashamed. You may be embarrassed to even just declare your passion. You'll almost certainly feel very vulnerable.

All normal. All OK. All not enough reason to keep it to yourself.

You can be as subtle as having your project on the table when people come over, or as dramatic as starting a blog and posting a link to it on Facebook. Take baby steps if it feels better, or just go big.

If you want to join a larger community of people who make stuff like the stuff you make, I highly recommend sharing your creations online instead of, or in addition to, sharing them in person. The easiest way is to post photos on a service like Instagram or Flickr, and use tags so your pics show up when people search for photos like yours. Or you can take a further step and start a Tumblr or a blog.*

Remember to take the important step of enabling people to find your posts by interacting with people who also share their creations.

It's OK if you express your concerns about sharing. People will understand, because everyone has been exactly where you are at one time or another. Just don't fall back on the unfair crutch of too much self-deprecation or fishing for compliments. Be honest. Be yourself.

A MORE DIRECTED APPROACH: If you're overwhelmingly intimidated, I get it. But you're not off the hook. Here are some very simple ways you can take the first steps of sharing:

* Be matter-of-fact about it. Write a post like this on Facebook: "I made a ___." That's it. Include a photo. If you're not making art or crafts, try something like, "I just wrote a short story (or a song or some choreography)." That's it.
* Let a picture tell a thousand words—just post one of your projects without saying anything at all. (Do your work justice and make sure you take a good picture of it. Use natural light and be sure to focus. Don't let a crappy picture make you or anyone else assume the object in it is also crap.)
* Mention it first on someone else's blog or Facebook page. If you have a favorite blogger or a friend whose creations you really admire, leave them a comment and tell them what you're making.

----

* I recommend using wordpress.com for blogging.

Keep in mind that even established artists and creators struggle with sharing. After a while, though, most people have experiences like the one Jasika Nicole had when she participated in a thirty-day drawing challenge (see page 126), posting a photo of a drawing on a particular theme every day: "Without having any kind of connection with an online forum, I am sure that I would have stopped the challenge sometime during week one. But there were so many people who kept commenting on my drawings every single day that I felt compelled to keep going, to stay true to my word. There have been drawings I wasn't proud of . . . but I posted every single image anyway, no matter my own personal feelings about it. My failures are just as important a part of me as my successes. I think that showing real-life vulnerability is a way to take out the 'mystery' of being a celebrity."

FLIP IT AROUND: Along with the creations you're proud of, show off your mistakes and failures.

"It's important to be aware that the self I share online is a highly edited version of myself. You're not getting the whole me, by any stretch of the imagination. However, I hope that if people met me, they wouldn't be too surprised by the offline me."

—KIRSTY HALL, ARTIST

No matter what other people do or say, *you* get to decide what and how much to share. Showing photos of the stuff you make does not mean you need to talk about your kids or your last dental appointment. Heck, you don't even need to use your real name. The goal of sharing your creations is to get them out of the vacuum of your mind and house and into the world. Anything else you share is entirely up to you. There's no right or wrong decision to make. And over time, you may feel that your decisions change. Go with it.

"If you're making anything creative, if you have a point of view about anything, someone is always going to disagree with you. If no one finds anything objectionable or worthy of critique in your work, you're making something so boring and milquetoast that it seems a stretch to call you a creator."

—ANN FRIEDMAN, JOURNALIST

On Criticism

I started following Ann Friedman's writing in 2012, when *GOOD* magazine, for reasons never well articulated but seemingly unrelated to their job performance, fired most of its editorial staff, including Ann, who was the executive editor. It wasn't her association with the dramatic gutting of a publication that drew me to her, it was that she and most of the people who were fired with her immediately turned around to create something awesome together. "So many people wanted to talk to us at that point in time, and mostly they were looking for us to give bitter quotes or anecdotes about being fired. Seeing as how we were all newly unemployed, we felt it was better to have a positive representation of our work—a future-oriented project—to direct the interview toward."

That future-oriented project was *Tomorrow*, a single-issue magazine Ann and her team crowd-funded through Kickstarter. They announced plans for the project within days of getting their pink slips, and as far as I could tell at the time, the story of their new-found unemployment never took a turn for the bitter. So when it comes to weathering serious public criticism and failure—while I'd argue that this case of being fired wasn't due to failure, being fired is certainly one of the harder forms of, shall we say, not succeed-ing—Ann is my hero.

Sure, very few of us maker-crafter-creative types are out to rock the boat, but I agree with Ann's quote on the previous page that any sort of original work, anything unique that's perceived not to have been done before, attracts lovers and haters alike. And though we may not strive to innovate, when we do, we do ourselves a favor to keep in mind that criticism—or its evil siblings, snark or trolling or bullying—only comes when we're making headway on doing something *new*.

And sometimes, a painful setback can be used as a springboard into doing something scary but amazing. As Ann says, "Sometimes it's nice to be forced to jump off that cliff, especially when you realize there's actually water underneath and not just rocks."

Since *Tomorrow*, Ann has been working steadily as a freelance journalist, and the rest of her team has found new work.

It's important to share our work and our thoughts and our ideas, even if some people hate it. And it's important that when we face down negativity or criticism or vicious setbacks, we do it with eyes on the future, with some trust that there will be cushions to land on.

WORST CASE SCENARIO: I ONCE HAD AN INTERNET NEMESIS*

Back in the days when I was still getting my feet wet with Crochet Me, I struck up a relationship with a new contributor to the online magazine. Eventually, that relationship soured. I found it very challenging when that happened. I'm outgoing and opinionated but not terribly keen on confrontation, and she got confrontational real fast. She called me names, asserted things about me that were patently false, and picked apart my work with a passion and energy that eventually became quite flattering but that initially broke my heart.

The reason she got to me, I realized after the initial shock wore off,** was that she voiced many of the things I was already very insecure about. She called me a fraud when I knew I was making things up as I went along (and hadn't yet gotten comfortable with that being a valid way of doing things). She tore apart my every decision and homed in on the exact factors I'd struggled with. She accused me of possessing qualities I loathe in others but secretly fear I exhibit. She accused me of being things I'm simply not, in

----

* I originally wrote about this on my blog in June 2013. Parts of this section were revised and updated from that post.

** That didn't happen quickly, by the way. It was weeks or months before I was able to gain any useful perspective on that whole situation.

ways that transcended personal insult and entered the realm of flagrantly offensive.

Over the years, I've spoken with a lot of makers and bloggers who have also had antagonistic relationships with someone online or face-to-face. These relationships are challenging, to say the least. And they can lead even the strongest, toughest-skinned people to want to quit rather than continue to repeatedly encounter such vitriol and pain. When your heart is breaking, it seems like a no-brainer to back away from the entire situation.

But keep in mind that a nemesis is just one person. Have you noticed that people rarely talk about nemeses? No. We normal, not-famous people don't have nemeses, in the plural. But anyone who shares anything personal, or voices any ideas that are different, or wishes publicly for something outside the mainstream, is likely to attract a reaction from about one person who doesn't know how to express herself except through hate.

This person and her words will cut right through our confidence and accomplishments and everyday balance and tip our whole world upside down. But we will right it all again. Because she's just one person, and she's expressing herself irresponsibly. Like the ugly voice in our own heads that we've been working hard to quiet, we will learn—through trial and painful error—to shield ourselves from the hate of the nemesis. It may take time, but it is always worth it. Always.

It's been several years since I've cared at all about my nemesis. I don't check in on her blog, even in the dark hours when I'm most vulnerable, and I don't have to stop myself from thinking about her when I'm anxious about work. I've healed. And I wouldn't change a thing about the experience. Having a nemesis was tremendously rewarding (in the end). I don't regret a single shed tear or sleepless night. It hurt like hell, but all important growing hurts like hell.

Before I had a nemesis, I cowered in the face of criticism. I was afraid of going too far or of getting it wrong or of offending someone. Because of my nemesis, I have a very clear understanding of the difference between criticism and snark; I welcome the former and roll my eyes at the latter. Because of my nemesis, I worked very hard to find my own voice and to accept the consequences of using it. Because of my nemesis, I'm comfortable trusting my gut, and I know that sometimes faking it till I make it is the best and most rewarding strategy to employ. Because of my nemesis, I feel comfortable taking visible risks, since the ugliest of ugly things have already been said about me. And even when she said those things, I couldn't help but notice that about six people agreed with her and everyone else didn't.

In many ways, my nemesis keeps company in my mind with the two or three people who have most dramatically influenced my career. That the other people were supportive rather than antagonistic doesn't make the strength of their influence any different.

Don't let a nemesis—or concern about attracting one—keep you from sharing your work, your ideas, and yourself. They're not worth it, and you are.

> **"People tend to hide behind their computers and not imagine the real-life person posting pictures of her work, so they feel like they can say whatever pops into their heads, and it used to hurt my feelings, and I'd want to respond back. I've since learned to laugh it off, and I really don't mind it."**
>
> —ALLISON HOFFMAN, CROCHET ARTIST

SECTION 3: THE CONTINUING BATTLE

THE DOLDRUMS

It inevitably sets in at some point—that feeling of ennui, the deep sigh of just plugging in one stitch after another, one more pen stroke, one more word. Don't beat yourself up about it; you haven't done anything wrong. You might just need a break, or a new project, or it may be time to shake things up in your routine.

When the doldrums set in for me, I've learned there's no use in forcing it. When I force myself to keep knitting, I make egregious mistakes. When I force myself to keep writing, I end up with drivel on the page and a sore tuchus from sitting too long. Sometimes I just need to binge on television or books, fill the tanks as Joss Whedon says (see page 163). I used to beat myself up for being a lazy sot, but I don't anymore. This is just the cycle that rules me, and I've learned to surrender to it. And I use this time to reach out to new things I've never done, since I can't possibly be tired of those, right?

In any case, I always end up returning to my true loves. Sometimes I just pick up where I left off; sometimes my hiatus leaves me with gifts I bring back to my projects, shifting them around a little. In either case, the detour is always worth it.

TRY SOMETHING NEW

FEAR OF FAILURE   PROCRASTINATION   BLOCK

I love knitting—it's the craft I have always turned to at the end of the day. But sometimes I just don't even feel like knitting. And at those times, I end up not making *anything*. Which is dumb. This exercise is to address those times when even the making you love just isn't doing it for you.

TRY MAKING SOMETHING YOU'VE NEVER MADE BEFORE.

Take a workshop. Visit a studio. Follow an intimidating recipe. Learn how to fix your leaky faucet. No commitment beyond just trying it out. If you have fun, great. If you hate it, fine. When you're done trying, go back to the stuff you know and love. Just see what it's like to inject some fresh air into your creative practice.

FLIP IT AROUND: Make something ugly. (What did you think I was gonna say?)

Breaking the Rinse, Repeat Cycle

I do not knit socks or mittens—knowing I'll complete one and then have to immediately make another one exactly like it stops me cold. It's hard enough to motivate myself to knit the second sleeve of a sweater. Add other people's expectations on top of my distaste for repetition, and you have the reason I've never considered making stuff for sale.

But even people who relish the rhythm of producing the same sort of item just for fun and not for profit occasionally find they need to change things up. Allison Hoffman is a crochet artist and designer who makes dolls that bear an uncanny resemblance to actual people, including celebrities. Some of her celebrity likenesses have received a lot of press, and her commissioned work is in high demand. It's not all fun, though, as she explains: "I sometimes feel pressure to keep producing the same stuff. Everyone wants another Doctor Who character, or they want me to make fifteen *Where the Wild Things Are* monsters for a birthday party, but what I really want to do is keep branching off into different directions and cover more ground."

When we become known for doing a particular thing very well—whether that renown takes the form of international fame or simply our friends applying the label to us—it can end up feeling quite stifling. "I want to take more risks," says Allison. "When I have to make something I'm not wholeheartedly interested in, or that I've made a hundred times, I tend to put it off. I feel completely bored with it all, and my work slows down a lot."

Back in Parts One and Two, it seemed like almost everything related to our creative experience was risky in one way or another. But now that you're in your groove, making your stuff and happily chugging along, it can be quite alarming to discover at some point that you're not enjoying it as much as you used to. *I've already done the work!* is what your brain might shout. And it's right, you have. But that doesn't mean you're not actually feeling a little bored or stuck or in a rut. Especially when other people seem to be counting on you to do your thing, changing things up, even just a little bit, can seem scary.

"I've had to learn to say 'no' more and more, which I find really difficult," Allison says, "but it has helped me get more control over doing what I want to do artistically and helps keep my work interesting. I've given up trying to make things everyone asks for, and I ask myself what's next now."

That might be easier said than done, but that doesn't mean it's not worth doing.

National Novel Writing Month (affectionately known by the worst acronym ever, pronounced phonetically: NaNoWriMo) takes place every November. The idea is to write a fifty-thousand-word novel in thirty days. The focus is on quantity over quality—to write that much in a month, participants are urged just to write write write. There's no time for second-guessing or revising; those can come later. It's a massive exercise in battling perfectionism and just writing the words. I've started twice but never completed my crappy novel. Maybe this year . . . Join me, won't you? www.nanowrimo.org.

P.S. Rachael Herron (read about how she makes time for her writing on page 138) wrote the draft of her first published novel during NaNoWriMo. True story.

READ A BOOK.
NO, A DIFFERENT ONE!

BLOCK

Most of the fuel we take in to power our creative life comes relatively quickly: a song, a show, a movie, a conversation, a walk, an essay, a poem. But books are another beast entirely. Reading a book is a commitment of time, so we tend to choose books we have good reason to believe we'll enjoy. We read a beloved author's entire body of work, we select from a particular genre over and over again, we get recommendations from friends who have similar taste. All of that is wonderful, and can provide exceptional enjoyment and occasional inspiration. But it doesn't really allow us to discover what we might be missing . . .

⇩ ⇩ ⇩

Along the lines of making new kinds of things when the doldrums set in, great value can be found in filling your head with different kinds of fuel too.

SO: READ A BOOK THAT'S NOT LIKE MOST OF THE BOOKS YOU READ.

That's it.

Die-hard fiction reader? Read a political autobiography. Love yourself some science books? Try a romance novel. Addicted to contemporary fiction? Read a graphic novel. Usually avoid books at all costs? Read any book.

(Sometimes, my ardent distaste for a book will cause me to throw it across the room before I finish the third chapter. Usually when this happens, I end up spectacularly inspired to make or write something of my own.*)

> Prolific film and television writer/director Joss Whedon spoke with *Fast Company* about how he gets so much done. "Fill the tanks, fill the tanks, fill the tanks. Constantly watch things and things you don't [normally watch]. Step outside your viewing zone, your reading zone. It's all fodder, but if you only take from one thing, then it'll show." Read more from the interview at bit.ly/whedon-prolific.

---

* I hope you're not about to throw this book across the room, but if you are, I hope you've found inspiration to go make something better.

PROMPTS -O- RAMA

PROCRASTINATION   BLOCK

Whether you're stuck because you're looking at a blank canvas or page, or you're in the throes of a project and your mojo grinds to a halt, prompts can sometimes deliver a swift kick in the pants.

I use prompts sometimes to get me going on a project that's stalled; I use them just to get my imagination going, period. Once that happens, I can usually walk away from the prompted work and miraculously see the struggling project with new eyes.

Prompts can serve as thematic constraints for writing and non-writing projects, alike. When I crochet monsters, I love to create a whole world for them in my imagination. Prompts help me flesh out a doll's personality, its history and motivation and dreams. Prompts help me stay silly, and silliness helps me not reject ideas too quickly.

⇩ ⇩ ⇩

Swirl your finger around in the air, then make it land at random on one of the following prompts. **IF THERE'S A BLANK, FILL IT IN. IF THERE'S A DIRECTION, FOLLOW IT. IF THERE'S A QUESTION, ANSWER IT. RINSE, REPEAT.**

* There's a hill over there. Go look on the other side of it. What do you see?

* It's three in the morning; there's a knock on your window.

* It is *freezing*. What do you do about it?

* That's not a monkey; it's a robot!

* Uh oh, the basement's flooded. What now?

* Use some yellow.

* Around the corner is an act of crime.

* And just then, you hear a babbling creek.

* Hey, what's in that secret notebook?

* That's not a sunrise; it's a sunset.

* How might this go better *without* a sprained ankle?

* Mmm. Delicious, delicious brains. These brains taste so _____.

* The music playing in the background is almost too loud to make out. You squint and hold on to the back of the bar stool and try to figure out why it sounds so familiar. You open your eyes and see them.

* There's a three-legged dog running down the middle of the street. You think _____.

* What would Buffy do?

* The coach is shouting in the dugout. You can't quite make out the words, but you think she's yelling _____.

* And then a cat saunters in.

* Add sparkle.*

* You need mountains in there.

* What will happen to the sea life?

* What if this all were happening in the nuclear winter?

* Hey, can you make that in yarn?

* Can this project be personified?

* How does it taste?

* Turn right ninety degrees.

* Inject some make-believe: a magic wand, a Pegasus, a space alien, a talking toad.

* Suddenly, it's all covered in gold.

* The raft starts to drift toward shore.

> Lauren Bacon recommends Brian Eno's "Oblique Strategies" cards for combatting block. Similar to this Prompts-O-Rama list of fairly absurd phrases and imperatives, each card in the deck includes a (not absurd) phrase intended to help you work through a creative dilemma. Learn more about them at bit.ly/oblique_strategies.

----

* Maybe not of the vampiric variety.

TRY THIS!

TAKE A WALK

PROCRASTINATION

BLOCK

It's a recurring thing, this whole "take a walk" idea, and for good reason. Especially when we're beating our heads against a problem that isn't moving no matter how hard we bang, a change of scenery and, more importantly, a shift in focus, can be the ticket to finding the solution.

There are loads of actual scientific research and tomes of anecdotal evidence that this works, so hit the Google if you doubt my insistence that this is a good idea.

But I'm just going to say it again: go take a walk. If it's raining, bring an umbrella. If it's snowing, wear warm boots. If it's the height of summertime, schmear on sunscreen. Step away from your desk or your table or whatever it is you're working on, and don't mentally bring the work with you. Leave it. It will not perish in your absence.

To help shift your focus, I'm going to assign you a task to complete. Even if this task doesn't lead you to bust through your block, it should be enjoyable enough not to feel like a waste of time. And let's face it: what you might actually need is a few days off, not an hour. It's up to you to recognize that need, and to give yourself permission to take that time off. If your own permission isn't enough, send me an e-mail, and I'll back you up on the permission front.

GO ON YOUR USUAL WALK. If your usual walk is to the bus stop on your way to or from work, that's your route. If you walk the dog every morning, that's your route. Whatever it is, just go about your usual walk. But give yourself a few extra minutes so you have time to take pictures of things, or to simply stand still and notice things. I do this every so often, and it's surprisingly refreshing.

Most mornings, I walk the dog in the woods near our house. I know the trails well, so I know which routes get me home faster on mornings when I need to rush, and I know how to take my sweet time if I can. Every so often, I follow a shorter route, but take my sweet time and document my walk with my phone's camera. I do it for no reason beyond how satisfying I find it to pay attention to details I usually don't notice because I'm lost in thought. Focusing on the environment around me gets me out of my head, and it allows me to appreciate my surroundings. I mean, I live a couple of blocks from amazing trails—that's something I don't take for granted. When I get home and look at my photos, I inevitably find them gorgeous, because they show me the beauty I usually fail to see. And I feel content to have spent some time just in those moments of my normal routine.

So take photos, or don't. Share them or delete them, it doesn't matter. Just enjoy your routine a little, for its own sake.

FLIP IT AROUND: Seek out the ugly or grotesque details. A rotting log, an overflowing garbage can, a neglected house.

When I can't stop myself from falling off a procrastination cliff, I turn to my own version of the Pomodoro Technique. It's my own version because I couldn't be bothered to read the documentation about this approach to productivity; after getting the overall gist, I've found it to be wildly effective. The idea is to set a timer for twenty-five minutes and work on a task, then take a five-minute break. It's surprisingly easy to do pretty much *anything* for twenty-five minutes. Most of the time I blow right past the timer too, and keep going. But I still try to remember to take regular breaks. Read more at www.pomodorotechnique.com.

SECTION 4: SUSTENANCE

THE RINSE, REPEAT CYCLE

You've established your creative rhythm, challenged your ugly voice, and battled your demons. Now it's time to enter the rinse, repeat cycle. You'll have highs and lows, your ugly voice will speak up again, demons will mount another offensive. You'll feel blocked sometimes and you'll procrastinate other times. Every new project will bring with it your old friends fear and doubt. Like I said in the very beginning, slain demons are only ever *mostly dead.*

This final section is about keeping your fuel tanks full of inspiration and motivation, and about pushing through the hard times while accepting that they're an inevitable part of creative life.

COLLABORATION

Much of this book, and most other books I've read about exploring creativity and combatting creative demons, focus on individual experience.* Some of my most satisfying creative spurts, though, have been spent with others. Creativity feeds off creativity, see, so don't avoid collaboration.

The experience I had experimenting with making mosaics that I wrote about in Part Two? I did complete one mosaic (ever). One night, my not-yet-husband—mosaic prodigy as he'd proven himself to be—and I decided to make a mosaic together. We took a twelve-inch-square piece of wood and sketched a basic shape of a sun to take up most of it, and then we drew a diagonal line from one corner of the board to the other. Greg tiled one half of the sun and I tiled

----

* A notable exception: Twyla Tharp's *The Collaborative Habit*, a follow-up to her outstanding book *The Creative Habit*.

the other. We didn't plan to work on it till the wee hours, but we did, sitting on the floor of our living room with a bottle of wine.

The resulting mosaic hangs in the entranceway to our house now. His half is more deftly executed with nicely cut tiles; mine contains more found objects like buttons and charms. The project didn't change our lives or our relationship, but it was exceptionally fun to do. It allowed us to appreciate our differences while working to create something only the two of us could make together.

Be sure to try collaborating every once in a while. You may create things you never knew you were capable of.

"Many of the best projects I have worked on (and those that have saved me in times of financial need) have come directly from friends I've met at conventions asking me to work with them."

—JOEL WATSON, CARTOONIST

Like the idea of collaborating but don't know where to begin? Here are some suggestions for how to get started:

* Develop a clear idea so you can convey it easily to potential collaborators. Saying, "I have this idea about making a twelve-foot-tall, animatronic papier-mâché goose for the next Maker Faire," is a lot more likely to garner support and collaboration than, "Hey, let's make something animatronic!"

* Avoid dismissing your idea out of hand. A twelve-foot-tall animatronic goose might sound ridiculous, but that doesn't mean it wouldn't be fun to make, and it could lead to other fulfilling projects.

* Listen to your instincts—to your gut—about whom to partner with. Your best friend might actually be a nightmare to share a project with, but that woman you met at the ceramics open house the other day might be exactly the one to approach.

* Start small—invite some friends over to work on a collaborative project like a quilt or other patchwork item that allows each person to work independently until all the pieces are put together.

* Start big—see above re: goose. Sometimes the boldness—even the *impossibility*—of an idea is exactly the thing to attract like-minded collaborators.

* Set a date—see if there are any community art challenges coming up (local arts- or crafts-supply stores might know about these kinds of events), and sign up with a friend; commit to building something for an event like a local Maker Faire, craft fair, or other event that's open to submissions; join in when your local guild or club hosts activities like a quilt-in, a knitting retreat, or a robot fight.

* Listen. People toss around ideas all the time, and if you listen carefully you'll be bound to discover some that you'll want to be a part of. All you'll have to do is speak up and say, "Yeah! Let's do it!" Then see where it goes.

* Be clear about your needs and expectations. Let your collaborators know if you only have limited time and/or money to put toward your project—avoid setting yourself up to feel stressed out or overwhelmed. And be clear about what your expectation is—will you push through to the end even if it turns out you're not having fun anymore? Or will you agree that this is a playful experiment, and if things get too difficult you can part ways amicably?

CROWDSOURCING HILARITY

This is the tale of an absurd idea and the dozens or hundreds of people who worked together to realize it. Collaboration can take any form, as long as more than one person is involved. This collaboration was pretty epic, and I'm sharing it here because I hope it proves to you that no idea is too silly, no limitation too absolute—if an idea makes your heart beat faster, you should try your hardest to work with whoever you can find to help you make it happen.

In the summer of 2008, Joss Whedon, whom you may now know as the director of the Hollywood smash hit *The Avengers* but who will always remain in my mind primarily the creator of the brilliant television shows *Buffy the Vampire Slayer* and *Firefly*, released a little project online.

Made without studio money and through calling in a lot of favors, *Dr. Horrible's Sing-Along Blog* is a forty-five-minute musical film about a wannabe villain, a hero jerk, and the girl they both love. Whedon released the film in three parts, online only, and initially for free. It was a very visible, very heavily publicized experiment in online media distribution from people who actually work in the mainstream entertainment industry.

One of the reasons Whedon has a vast and passionate fan base is that he gives great interviews. He's funny and candid and notoriously sarcastic. In an interview with *Wired* magazine that summer,[*] he was asked how media coverage for *Dr. Horrible* was going, and he replied, "Fact is, there's been some buzz, but it hasn't reached the places it would normally. Where's our write-up in *Crocheting Monthly*? (I did a very sexy shoot for that one.)"

At the time, I was the editor of a crochet magazine and I ran a huge crochet website. It's possible I was the only person in North

----

[*] See bit.ly/drhorriblewired.

America who could provide Whedon this write-up. And if I wasn't, it's at least quite likely I was the only one who wanted to.

After some hilarious chats with crafty Whedon fans,* we launched a campaign to attract his attention. It was absurd and hilarious. The idea was to make some noise and see if we could make the interview happen.** We asked people to post photos of crafts they'd made inspired by Whedon shows and comics. We asked people to ask around in the hopes that someone would know someone who might know someone connected to his work.

Meeting so many enthusiastic crafters made the whole thing fun—I'd had no idea so many crafters are also geeks like me! I mean, if you were to get a few dozen crafters in a room and yell out "Jane Austen and The Doctor would make a perfect couple!" I'd bet big money that a great and passionate argument would ensue. But beyond the enjoyment of getting our crafty geek on, it was truly amazing when we started getting some traction. Major entertainment blogs picked up our effort, and they didn't even make fun of it.

And it turned out my husband's cousin was in a playgroup with someone who knew a frequent Whedon collaborator. And an avid Whedon fan dug up some old contact information. And one of my college roommates worked at an entertainment magazine and alerted her colleague, who had organized panel discussions with Whedon and crew. In the end, the formal connection came from a crochet designer I worked with whose cousin is a comic-book artist and had once eaten lunch with the artist who drew the covers of the *Buffy* comics. He said she was friendly, and he'd reach out.

----

* My dear friend Elin provided all the initial encouragement I needed to pursue this idea. She hunted down Whedon's official agency contact information and e-mailed it to me, thus taking two snowflakes and sending them down a mountain until they turned into the avalanche that followed.
** See the original blog post here: bit.ly/geekcrafters.

A week or two later, my colleague got an e-mail from Whedon's assistant—Joss definitely wants to do the interview, she wrote, but he's very busy taping his new series, *Dollhouse*; we'll be in touch.

This whole series of events? The most fun I've had online, to date. There was nothing to lose. A crochet website wanting to interview a Hollywood director! Hilarious. And I also felt that *I* had nothing to lose. If I failed at making the interview happen, so be it. My ugly voice, ordinarily inclined to tell me I'm a loser for loving some television shows too much, and usually so vehement in its insistence that nobody would want to join me in such a harebrained crusade, was entirely drowned out by my manic giggles and shouts of glee.

Every few weeks I'd send Whedon's assistant an e-mail letting her know we were still interested, no rush.

Then one day in November—four months after we established this plan—I heard back from her. She could give me a half-hour phone call with him the next day or three days later. That's when the panic hit. I wonder if she heard how high-pitched and strained my voice was through e-mail. I requested the later date.

Over the next few days, I collected question suggestions from crafty geeks, I bought a microphone, and Diane Gilleland of the sadly now-discontinued Craftypod podcast gave me a crash course in recording a phone conversation on my computer.

With my giggles and shouts giving way to planning and planning some more, some serious doubts crept into my thinking. What on earth was I doing? This man will certainly know I'm a hack. And all the crafters! People are so excited, and I'm a hack who will surely let them down. They'll hate me and I'll look like a fool and I'm sure I'll screw up the electronics and . . .

Eventually, I just had to take a deep breath, punch my ugly voice in his adorable green face, and dial the number.

I learned some things while speaking with Joss Whedon on the phone. My voice really does reach astonishing heights when I'm nervous. It's not a good idea to have your microphone on the same surface as your computer if the computer's fan will be whirring while you record. Best to record each voice on a separate track, for ease of editing. Joss Whedon is as kind and generous and funny as you'd think he'd be from other interviews.

So the recording of the interview was abysmal. The fan whirring obscured Whedon's voice enough to make some of his words unintelligible. In the end, rather than just posting the recording as a podcast as I'd planned, I spent hours and hours transcribing the conversation.

And you know what? Not one person complained about the audio quality, everyone just read the text. Even non-crafty Whedon fans enjoyed the crafty conversation we had. Working together, the geeky crafts community achieved the unlikely and the wonderful. We were graced by Whedon with gems like this, about knitting and crochet: "It's an age-old war. Like the werewolves and the vampires. I think *Underworld* was actually originally about crocheters and knitters, but they thought it would be too controversial, so they changed it to vampires and werewolves."*

I'd had so much fun with these shenanigans, it highlighted for me why I love being a freelancer doing creative work. It hammered home to me that I thrive on spontaneity and absurdity. I realized I'm unhappy without independence and the possibility of spur-of-the-moment projects that take over my life. From that point forward, I

----

* You can read the transcribed interview at bit.ly/whedoncrafts or in the book *Joss Whedon: Conversations*, edited by David Lavery and Cynthia Burkhead.

knew that I wouldn't have an opportunity to get bored with my work if I crafted my work to be endlessly challenging and new. And, perhaps most importantly, I learned how very important it is to keep in touch with my people. I need to collaborate with people who are also inclined to do silly things, harebrained things, unusual things, and to have fun even when falling flat on our collective face.

It's not like I routinely throw blog parties now to try to gain media attention. But I keep in mind that when I work with people who are passionate about things like I'm passionate, good things happen.

FEATURETTE

On Just Doing It

One of the things Joss Whedon said during our interview has stayed with me since. We were discussing how the internet and other rapidly advancing technologies now enable absolutely anyone to make and distribute video projects, and he said, "It is no longer the time of sitting around and thinking about doing something."

It used to be that an ambitious idea required the support of others—a film studio, a publisher, a patron, a grant. But right now, most projects can be executed without jumping those daunting hurdles. I'm not saying that film studios and publishers and granting agencies have lost their usefulness, not at all. But I am saying that they're no longer a necessary component to creating things and getting them out into the world.

I'm a starter of projects (not so much a finisher). It's how I roll. And sometimes I get so excited, so completely enamored and overwhelmed by the potential of a project, that just that excitement is enough to get me out of bed in the morning. I can spend hours upon consecutive hours daydreaming about doing this idea I have. I can

continued

talk about it as if it's already done. But what I'm actually doing is a whole lot of nothing.

Cartoonist Joel Watson echoes Whedon's sentiment. Joel writes a web comic called *HijiNKS ENSUE*, and when he decided to pursue the project as his full-time work he was, and continues to be, unusually honest with his readers about the financial risk he was taking. In doing so, he provides a real-life example of what's involved in running a solo creative business.

He summed up the task like this: "Just start making your thing. Stop planning for the end result (freedom, financial independence, creative fulfillment), and start doing the work. Start today. Start right now. Make the thing you want to make, and put it out there without hesitating. Chances are you are going to hate the first thing you make in a year, regardless. Get that part out of the way. Stop talking about how you want to or wish you were doing something creative and just get started. Then go find more people doing that same thing and talk to them. Put yourself where they are, be it online or in person. If the creative community you want to be a part of isn't welcoming you with open arms, start a new one. **GO GO GO, DO DO DO, MAKE MAKE MAKE,** because eventually you are going to die and this is your only chance to be happy."

Truth.

TRY THIS!

FIND
YOUR PEOPLE

SELF-DOUBT

We have not lived for very long in the age of online social media. Because these tools still feel so new to us, they're frequently decried as catalyzing the end of civilization. Luddites and curmudgeons throw their hands in the air and talk about kids these days who don't know how to talk on the telephone anymore and who never see their friends in person and who will certainly grow up to be antisocial adults who will fail to participate in society, thus rendering us all to a gruesome demise amidst disease and anarchy.

Since we all know that won't actually happen—I mean, the telephone was also predicted to bring down society when it was invented— let's spend some time thinking about our people.

Community plays a vital role in our lives, and it's important beyond our neighborhood and church/synagogue/mosque experiences. We have specific interests that can be nurtured and fueled by others who share similar interests. Connecting with our special-interest communities, if you will, is an outstanding way to fuel creative practice. And we don't have to connect with these communities in person if we can't or simply don't want to (see that? I'm saying here that online community is the same as in-person community).

If I had to name one way the internet has most profoundly influenced daily life, I'd say it's the way it's brought people together. I bet there was an editorial in your local paper just last week about how social media are ruining society and making us dumb and psychotic, written by an arm-waving curmudgeon. I just don't buy it.

Social-media expert Alexandra Samuel delivered a TEDxVictoria talk called "Ten Reasons to Stop Apologizing for Your Online Life," in which she asserts that our online relationships and activities are as much "real life" as our relationships and activities offline. I know in my own experience, my offline creative life is enhanced tremendously by my online relationships and conversations, and vice versa. Watch at bit.ly/ online-life.

The niche communities online that connect people from all over the world in their passion for a common interest bring us together in ways that were simply impossible before this technology existed. It's what made Crochet Me magical for me—meeting people I never, ever would have met otherwise and forming close friendships that started because we shared an interest in crochet and crafts. This magical internet thing doesn't only happen with crafters, obviously. It happens with people who are interested in absolutely anything, from vintage comics to science-fiction television to running marathons. Especially for shy people, meeting fellow geeks online can be earth-shattering in all the best of ways. Naturally, the same communities exist in person—if not in your tiny town, then at least in the bigger city nearby. Regardless of how you meet them, and whether you meet them face-to-face or only in pixels, knowing people who share your interests or experiences is powerful and rewarding. Especially when you get to know people who struggle with similar challenges as you.

Also, knowing like-minded folks can soften the blow when you tell your Muggle friends and family what you're up to and they stare at you blankly.*

Whether through Google or the Yellow Pages or just asking around, try to find a local group or community hub for an interest you have. Then show up. Here are some tips to make this less awkward or intimidating:

* When you find a group that looks good, see if they have an e-mail newsletter you can subscribe to. This will allow you to get a feel for the personalities behind the group and the stuff they do. If it still looks good to you after a few weeks, sign up for or show up to one of their events.
* Find some blogs related to your interest. When something strikes your fancy or strikes a chord, leave a comment. Over time, you may be able to forge a relationship with the blogger.

----

* I do so love my Muggle friends and family, and I don't value their relationships less because they're Muggles; I've just learned to save my proper geeking out for times I'm with fellow geeks, know what I mean?

- Use www.meetup.com to find casual gatherings of interest groups in your area.
- Stop into a shop related to your interest and see if they hold events or know of any local groups. Small one-off shops are best for this; big-box stores tend not to be hubs of community (though I'm sure there are exceptions). I know of many yarn, fabric, comics, and gaming shops that occupy the center of their respective communities.
- Attend events. Craft fairs, exhibit openings, Maker Faires, and studio open houses attract people just like you. So do poetry readings, open mic nights, author readings, and street fairs.
- Volunteering is a great way to get to know people faster and more intimately than if you were to just run into them from time to time at events. Find an event you love and volunteer to help put it on. It's a guaranteed way to meet people who are as dedicated as you are and to learn about all sorts of other related things to do.
- Take a class. If your interest is purely intellectual because you've never done the thing, step away from YouTube tutorials and take a class where you'll have a chance to meet other beginners in your area. Many a knitting group was born from a beginner knitting class. I know, I know, "Go take a class!" is like the ultimate generic advice for finding new people to connect with. But it really is especially practical for someone like you, who has a clearly identified interest you want to pursue. Go do it, and meet people who are also interested in that thing.

GUT FEELINGS

I used to think hunches were the exclusive purview of cops, private detectives, and scientists.

Then I realized that the way I feel when I'm trying to force my square self into a round hole is an actual physical sensation. I feel it in my gut, just like the saying goes.

Listening to my gut is a skill I'm still working on. It used to be that I'd only notice it when I was doubled over in pain—only then would I realize I was going down a path that was very, very wrong. I'd be left to backtrack, and in doing so I'd feel relief, but I'd also leave a trail of unmet commitments, and my ugly voice would have a field day telling me I was doing what I'd gotten so good at doing—bailing, quitting, not following through. I wouldn't notice my gut when it was screaming at me to do it, either. I was very good at talking myself out of opportunities, despite my gut telling me I shouldn't pass them up.

If you're not enjoying what you're making, stop making it. It's OK to hate knitting even if your beloved grand-mother taught you how. It's OK to leave a project in the corner for a year (or forever) if it makes you miserable. It's also OK to follow your gut feeling that you'll love painting—go buy the brushes and paints and canvases even if you've never actually painted before. It's OK to take a dance class when you're over forty. It's OK to travel to Mexico to learn how to make a burrito.

It's OK, it's OK, it's OK.

Now, though, I'm able to listen to my gut while I'm still making a decision. About some things, my insides really do twist themselves up, and if I don't heed that warning, I end up regretting it in a big way. My gut alerts me to the things I know but don't want to accept—like that collaborating with certain people might end up more painful than fruitful (even if I really like them and admire their work), or that I'm considering a commitment I'm not excited enough about to complete without complaint. My gut also tells me about positive things—it spreads a sparkly happy feeling through my veins when I'm faced with a choice that can be amazing but might not make logical sense.

Regardless of the situation, my gut is *always right*. When I've ignored its warnings, I've ended up unhappy *every single time*. And when I've heeded its sparkly promises, I've had tremendous fun, or accomplished terrific feats, or both.

Austin Kleon, author of the brilliant book *Steal Like an Artist*, delivered a Creative Mornings talk during which he gave some very simple, very good advice. Pay particular attention to what he says about sharing his work at bit.ly/austin-kleon-cm.

Creative Mornings is a monthly speaker series that started in New York City and is spreading rapidly to cities all over the world. Once a month, people gather to eat breakfast and hear a twenty-minute talk related to creativity. Look for a chapter in your city (or start one!) at www.creativemornings.com.

On a more granular scale, my gut also has opinions about how I should proceed with a particular project, and its opinions are as unrelated to objective logic as they are when it comes to huge life decisions. I'll usually know within a few rows if a knitting project is going to be beloved or loathed, just based on how I feel making the first stitches. When I ignore an icky feeling, the project inevitably ends up languishing in a corner. When I'm designing a project from scratch, I'll spend quite a bit of time sketching and planning and measuring and doing math. I won't pick up my hook and yarn until I'm confident I'll just have to follow my own instructions. Naturally, it never goes as smoothly as I'd planned, and it's my gut that induces all the changes I end up making. My brain will see only sense and logic—that my numbers add up and so the result should look perfect. My gut will insist that what I'm looking at ain't perfect at all, that in fact it desperately needs some rethinking, and maybe some new colors, and possibly starting entirely from scratch.

Do you have gut feelings? When do you notice them? And how do you handle them? Do you follow your gut or try to ignore it?

Betz White turned me on to one of my favorite books, *The Universal Traveler: A Soft-Systems guide to creativity, problem-solving and the process of reaching goals,* by Don Koberg and Jim Bagnall. Originally published in 1972, the workbook-size handbook is filled with wisdom and inspiration like this gem:

"It's unreasonable to imagine escaping fear altogether. But by changing your focus from 'I'm afraid to be wrong' to 'I'm trying to be right,' the positive point of view can help in overcoming this major block to a more creative life."

The very dated, very obviously cut-from-paper-and-pasted-with-glue zine-like book is itself a reminder that none of our struggles is new, or unique to us. Yes, I believe *The Universal Traveler* is my favorite book of all.

This is not the same thing as your ugly voice. The ugly voice plays a very specific role in supporting your demons—it's *always* going to say negative things to you, it will always try to knock you down. Your gut is more like a physical connection to your own mind—it expresses to you what's at the heart of how you feel about something, whether it's a color choice or a major job decision. For some, it's like a moral compass; for others, it's like an aesthetic barometer. I've come to think of my gut feelings as a special confidante, who often knows me better than I know myself. Where the ugly voice often lies, or at the very least illuminates our own worst fears, the gut tells us the truth. It's our own internal Magic 8 ball.

Try to listen to it, try to notice what it's saying to you. Get a feel for what your gut feelings are when you're making stuff, and when you're deciding what to do with the stuff you make.

FEATURETTE

On Red Flags and Going for It

Betz White is a sewing pattern designer and author who has pointed me toward many of my favorite resources related to creative practice. Because she's so thoughtful about her creative experience, I wasn't at all surprised when she told me about a time she ignored her gut and it didn't go very well.

"Once, I was asked to contribute to a group project that was out of my comfort zone," she told me. "I felt a bit intimidated by the other participants who were well known in an industry that I was only on the fringe of. I was honored to be asked, yet my gut was waving a red flag. In the end, I'm proud of my contribution from a personal-growth standpoint, but my finished project was not on par with the others."

It's hard to balance advice we're given against how we might feel about an individual problem or opportunity. Admonitions to "get out of your comfort zone!" are ubiquitous, it seems, but as with any advice, it's not *always* good to take it. Most of the time, the only tool we have to figure out whether advice is best taken or ignored is our gut.

Betz certainly didn't ruin her career by pursuing that project despite her gut's protestations, and she did learn some hard lessons she's kept in mind since. I think these lessons are better to keep in mind than blanket statements that aren't always helpful. In Betz's words: "Stretch yourself, but trust your gut! Don't let someone else's confidence or motives sway your decisions. Learn to say no sometimes, and be OK with that. Never put anything out there that does not live up to your own standards."

TRY THIS!

GO BIG

FEAR OF FAILURE   SELF-DOUBT

The most exciting projects I've ever done were born from fear, audacity, and deliberate ignorance. By which I mean I bit off more than I could chew. I said *yes* before thinking. I said *yes* after thinking I was wholly unqualified or unprepared. I committed to my own idea without allowing time for second-guessing, questioning how I'd follow through, or worrying about the consequences.

Granted, I haven't done this *all the time*. To do this all the time would be reckless and dumb. But when my gut screams *yes*, I follow it even if my brain says *maybe not*.

And on the flip side, I've held myself back at times I really shouldn't have. Like the first garment I ever knitted was a poncho with fun-fur accents. Oh yes, it was. I made it because I believed that it would be a good intermediate step between the scarves I'd knitted and tackling a sweater. But you know? I didn't *need* the intermediary step, just like I certainly didn't need that poncho. I didn't learn anything I didn't already know, and I didn't particularly enjoy the project, either.

So here's to being audacious and just doing the big thing. You should try it.

This is a different sort of exercise because it's not (necessarily) one you can just start doing right now. You'll have to wait for an opportunity (which doesn't mean you shouldn't or couldn't work to create such an opportunity).

When that opportunity arises, here's how it might go:

* You might double-check to see that you're the correct recipient of the e-mail or phone call. Clearly they must have meant to ask someone else.
* You'll probably blush. Or sweat.
* You may immediately move to decline politely by saying things like you're not qualified, or that you're flattered but just can't, or that you know someone who's better suited to the project. You will almost certainly feel the cold stone of terror in your gut.

When something like this happens, **DO THIS EXERCISE.** Go ahead and rip these pages out of the book and fold them into your wallet so you'll have them handy at all times, since stuff like this usually comes without warning.

OK, this is the exercise:

WAIT JUST A MINUTE.

Pause. Just, hold on.

DON'T SAY OR DO ANYTHING YET.

Take a step back and forget your humility. Put yourself into the shoes of the person who's approached you and try to see what they see. Try to see why they asked you. Sure, they may have asked other people before you, but you're on their list, kid. Do you think any Oscar-winning actor feels they don't deserve the award because they weren't the director's first choice for the role?

Think around the stone-cold terror in your gut and see if there's anything else swimming around in there. Rays of hope? Pride? Some fear of the sort that's the best to embrace? Demons worth slaying?

If you see any of those things, if you feel excited, just hold on another minute.

Those are signs this is the kind of opportunity to take. When your discomfort is coupled with wonder or excitement or that special kind of curiosity about how it would feel to totally nail it, chances are the discomfort you'll feel will be worth it. As the great Wayne Gretzky said, "You'll always miss 100 percent of the shots you don't take."

So close your eyes and look ahead a few decades. What do you see? Did you do it? Did it shift your path closer to the one you wanted to be on? Are you proud of yourself for what you decided, whether yes or no?

OK, now reply.

I asked Lauren Bacon what kinds of advice she gives people when they're struggling specifically with their business demons. Here's what she said:

> Talk about it with other entrepreneurs who've been there. Compare notes. Entrepreneurs have a terrible tendency to hole themselves up and believe everyone else's press releases rather than finding out the story behind the scenes—and we compare our challenging experiences with other people's success stories.
>
> The upside to that is that we're always striving, which is generally a good thing, but the downside is that we tend to beat ourselves up unnecessarily.
>
> Mentors, coaches, mastermind groups, really good conferences are all critical tools to help you find trusted community and figure out your own path.
>
> It's also crucial that you figure out what success looks like for you. Set aside everybody else's definitions, and actually write down (or draw, or whatever method works for you) how you'll know when you're successful. What kind of revenue do you want? What kind of work will you be doing? How much time off, travel, flexibility, social vs. non-social time do you want to have? Really think hard about all of that stuff because otherwise, you end up inheriting other people's ideas of what success looks like, and you never really feel successful or satisfied.

Also, see Arianna Huffington's 2013 Smith College commencement address for her thoughts on redefining success to prioritize meaning and health in addition to wealth and fame at bit.ly/huffington-commencement.

On Diving In

The documentary film *Handmade Nation*, released in 2009, was like a housewarming party for a generation of crafters. Filmmaker Faythe Levine had never made a documentary before, but doing something like taking on the gargantuan task of documenting the resurgence of the indie crafts scene in the United States wasn't new to her. For years, she put on the Art vs. Craft event in Milwaukee, and every year she applied some obvious logic to combat her recurring concern that no one would attend: "It's like the thought of having a party where no one shows up; it just can't happen."

She didn't dismiss the fear; she just explained it away. "The looming **WHAT IF** no one comes is always gut-wrenching, until the end of the day when we've discovered over four thousand people showed up."

So when it came to making *Handmade Nation*, she just showed up and did it. "I dove in headfirst with little to no idea about what was going to unfold. I am fairly stubborn about finishing something I start, so almost three years later I was able to look back and know it was the best thing I could have done with myself during those years."

Going big doesn't always have to involve major projects; it can be about taking a simple but audacious risk too. Artist Stacey Rozich told me about the first time she approached an editor about featuring her art:

"I was guided by a fear of rejection for most of my younger life as an artist, I was paralyzed by the idea of someone seeing my work—which I regarded as the purest and most vulnerable form of myself—and laughing at me and dismissing it as garbage. In my early twenties, I was an avid reader of a San Francisco art blog that I became obsessive about checking; it showcased new up-and-coming artists whom I admired and envied. I dreamed of seeing my work on this website too, but I couldn't see how it would ever be possible. Finally, one day on a whim, I mustered up my courage and sent the editor my blog for him to look over. I instantly regretted my bold move because I knew it would never be seen. But then, almost immediately I got an e-mail back asking for a feature and interview with me on this very site. It ended up being a really great jump-starter for my career, and I am eternally grateful for it even still."

Nothing horrible would have happened if Stacey hadn't heard back from that editor. She may have continued to be afraid, and she may have waited a long time before approaching someone again. But all she had to do when she heard back was say yes.

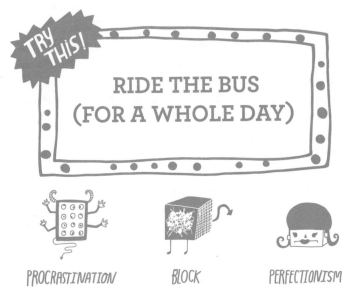

RIDE THE BUS
(FOR A WHOLE DAY)

PROCRASTINATION   BLOCK   PERFECTIONISM

Despite the plethora of pithy exercises throughout this and many other books, sometimes what your creative soul needs is a whole lot of nothing. We don't have much nothing in our lives, and we'd do ourselves a world of good to insert some occasionally. This exercise is intended to give you nothing. In all the best of ways.

This is a whole-day activity, but it isn't a chore and shouldn't seem like one, so don't fret about using a day off for it. In fact, you may want to take a day off for it. I'd bet money you'll be glad you did.

Here's what you do:

ON A DAY WHEN YOU'RE ABLE TO FREE YOURSELF FROM COMMITMENTS, RIDE THE BUS. If your neighborhood isn't connected to a bus line, drive to the nearest town or city with a half-decent transit system. (Take note of how late the buses run [if the nearest transit system is sub-par, I'd hate for you to end up stranded somewhere when the buses stop running at 6:00 p.m.].)

Bring a book or your knitting or a magazine or nothing at all. If you need a safety net, bring a map or make sure your smartphone is fully charged. Now set out on a day of meandering.

Get off the bus at a park that looks inviting. Walk around it. Sit on a bench and read your book or knit your knitting. Get back on the bus.

Get off when you see a cafe and realize you're starving. Ask the server what they recommend for lunch.

Get back on the bus and ask the driver what he or she recommends as a good stop for exploring. Hopefully you live in a place where you won't be given the stinkeye for conversing with the driver. If you do, find a friendly looking passenger and ask them.

Go to the museum you always plan to go to but something always comes up.

Go to the library.

When you find yourself near a friend's house, stop in for a few minutes to say "hi."

Get back on the bus.

Continue until you're bored. Hopefully you'll do a good job of keeping yourself entertained, but maybe this isn't really up your alley. So be it. The goal is to not have a destination, and to allow yourself enough unstructured time to enjoy the journey.

FLIP IT AROUND: Stop in places you usually avoid because they make you uncomfortable (I'm not talking about *unsafe*).

The Helsinki Bus Station Theory is a fascinating approach to considering commitment and dedication to learning your art or craft. As the title of this article about it states, it may just change your life: bit.ly/HelsinkiBus.

GO FAR, FAR AWAY

My favorite travel experience was when I spent a week in Tokyo. I've never been anywhere more different from home than that massive city. No one paid any attention to the sweaty North American walking around clueless and curious. In one of the largest cities in the world, I felt beautifully alone. Not stranded, not lonely, just able to take from my travels what I would. I'm sure I'd feel disoriented if I were to stay longer, but just for that week, I enjoyed every minute (and every meal).

Travel can be the most potent fuel for creativity. A walk around town or a bus trip to an unfamiliar neighborhood can be refreshing or inspiring, but getting far away from home can be downright revolutionary. Travel whenever you can. Take copious notes, make sketches, take pictures. Smell the smells and see the sights and, most importantly, talk to locals.

WHEN QUITTING IS JUST MOVING ON AT THE RIGHT TIME

Being overwhelmed is a normal part of life. How we handle it relates intimately with how gracefully we're able to navigate the unexpected twists and turns that always seem perfectly timed to create chaos and misery.

There are times I'm convinced my world is run by Murphy and all his stupid laws. At least a couple of times a year, one minor setback ends up being followed by another setback, which is followed by a sudden illness, which is followed by the car breaking down, which is followed by the dog barfing on my fabric stash, which is followed by my kid not sleeping well, which is followed by the coffeemaker breaking. When this kind of avalanche of crap descends, there's simply no way I can follow through with all of my regular plans and obligations. So at times like these, I do a very quick, very decisive evaluation of what I like to think of as the low-hanging fruit of my life.

The fruit at the top of the metaphorical tree, the hard-to-reach stuff, are commitments that are too complicated, painful, or unthinkable to put off, cancel, or otherwise alter. The lower on the tree the fruit is, no matter how important or exciting it seemed the day before, the more comfortable I feel letting go. When my brain feels like a nuclear reactor about to melt down, jettisoning this low-hanging fruit is like injecting some coolant to stave off catastrophe. It's at times like these that maintaining a creative habit is the hardest.

Sometimes the lowest-hanging fruit is social plans, sometimes it's far-off work commitments, sometimes it's promises to myself. It's the creative promises to myself that are the most complicated to consider. I can easily assess the probable effect of bailing on a lunch date with a colleague (happens all the time; she'll understand). And it's pretty straightforward to project the consequences of turning down a minor work contract, especially if I have other prospects or know the client well. But my personal creative commitments, well, those are commitments to myself. That makes them seem like the most obvious choices to jettison, since they won't affect anyone but me.

Here's the thing, though. All those adages asking who will take care of the caretaker are rooted in truth. If the first things we sacrifice in this unending cycle of overwhelmingness are our personal commitments, we'll end up a puddle of misery, and we won't be very good at handling these frequent difficult situations anymore. It's not selfish to spend time on our creative obligations—and it's not selfish to consider our creative desires to be obligations.

I used to see quitting—or bailing or jettisoning or postponing—as failure, and I just don't see it that way anymore. OK, yes. Sometimes quitting is failing. Because quitting *prevents* you from failing, and failing is important. We learn from failing. We learn so very, very much from it. And so quitting means you take away that opportunity to learn. But following through with absolutely everything is not a recipe for success. Quitting the things whose failures wouldn't be valuable is called taking care of yourself.

TRY THIS!

WRITE ME A LETTER

FEAR OF FAILURE   SELF-DOUBT   PERFECTIONISM

PROCRASTINATION   BLOCK

I began this particular exercise with subscribers to my e-mail newsletter,* and it's been so rewarding—for letter-writers, to get things off their chest; and for me, to know I'm not alone and to feel trusted as a confidant—I think it's the perfect final exercise in this book.

In my younger days, and, in fact, well beyond the introduction of e-mail into my daily life, I used to write a lot of letters. Though I never had a formal pen pal, one blessing of moving far way every so often was that I left good friends behind. So where in high school

----

* You should get it! Subscribe at bit.ly/kw-newsletter.

I'd ignore my teachers by writing lengthy notes to my best friend whom I'd see in half an hour, as I got older I'd ignore my professors by writing letters I'd send through the mail to people I trusted with my most verbose thoughts.

At some points in my early-adult development, these letters became like a kind of semi-public diary for me. In telling another human being what I was thinking and feeling, I felt I accomplished something I couldn't achieve through keeping a journal only for myself (I did keep a journal for quite a long time too).*

Some confessions had to pass beyond my own eyes in order for me to properly confront myself. I needed the perspective. Even if my friend never wrote back, I needed to have the experience of examining myself from what I anticipated might be their perspective. (In my imagination, my friends were always easier on me than I was on myself, even when they called me on my BS.) And I needed to feel, sometimes, like I got things off my chest. I needed to share the burden.

When you get to a point when you feel you're carrying a burden—of shame, of confusion, or feeling blocked or uninspired—do this exercise. Just the act of confessing, of being brutally honest about your struggle, can be cathartic. At the very least, you'll unload some of the tremendous weight you're carrying around.

⇩ ⇩ ⇩

WRITE ME A LETTER. Write me a letter about the fear or worry or discomfort you feel regarding your creativity—about making things, about making money from creative pursuits, about perfectionism,

---

* I've gotten back into journaling recently.

about judgment, about frustration, about failure, about shame. Even as you berate yourself for having come this far, and how, dammit, you should be able to handle this on your own by now, give yourself permission to ask a stranger for help. Just do it. Unload.

Send me the letter. I will not judge you. I will not roll my eyes at you. I will not think you're being ridiculous.

If you tell me to, I'll destroy the letter after I read it and never mention it to a soul.

If you give me permission to, I might write about your letter on my blog or elsewhere, and perhaps other people who are struggling will know they're not alone (I can do this anonymously or by crediting you—whichever you indicate).

Take half an hour or three hours or five minutes. Get it off your chest. Before you can convince yourself you're being stupid or silly or that you're whining to a stranger, SEND IT. Lick the envelope and slap a stamp on it (remember your postage needs to get your letter to Canada).

Address it to:

Kim Werker
P.O. Box 45536
Westside R.P.O.
Vancouver, BC V6S 2N5
CANADA

Now, go make something.

Final Thoughts

Remember way back when you stuck a list of your hero qualities up on your bedroom wall or dog-eared the page so you could look at it when you needed to be reminded of your strength? Well, I hope you're feeling even stronger now that you've reached these final pages.

I also hope that you're not expecting your adventure to be over. Surely you've noticed—or at least noted that I keep saying—that the demons never fully die. That's not because you keep failing in your battles; it's just life. Highs and lows and all the mediums in between.

But now you're better equipped to slog through the hard battles and enjoy the flow during the good times. Now you know you *can* slog through, that it's worth it, that there's satisfaction and happiness on the other side.

REMEMBER THAT UGLY IS MIGHTY

Fear, doubt, perfectionism, procrastination, block, and all the shades of demons between and around them—they'll be a part of your creative practice forever. Remember what you've accomplished on these pages. Remember that those demons aren't plaguing you because you suck, or because you're untalented, or because you shouldn't be trying. Remember that they plague you because you're human, just like they plague your neighbors, just like they plague the artists and musicians and crafters and makers and performers whose work electrifies and inspires you.

Remember how valuable ugly is. When you get to a point when you feel like a caged animal, remember that making something ugly can be the master key to get you out. It can help you see clear paths where before you only saw dead ends; it can help you see color where before you saw only gray. If nothing else, it'll keep your hands busy for an hour and hopefully free your mind.

Remember that your struggles mean you're onto something—even if that something requires an about-face. Trying to pretend those struggles aren't important won't get you anywhere but stuck. So look at them, immerse yourself in them, no matter how uncomfortable it feels. Then slay some demons, have a long chat with your ugly voice, and move on to make more stuff.

Finally, remember to relish the great times. Remember to accept and savor compliments, to feel proud of your accomplishments, to delight in the thrill of achievement. Take credit when it's yours to take, and give it liberally.

FEATURETTE

The Importance of Duality

One day, tooling around online in a geek fangirl maelstrom of open browser tabs, I discovered that the actor who played Astrid on the sci-fi show *Fringe* keeps a Tumblr blog. And so I discovered one of my favorite blogs.

Jasika Nicole does everything, it seems. She knits; she sews; she draws; she's achieved some awesome feats in upholstery. But more than her crafts, I love her approach to making things. She just seems to love it so much, and she rarely qualifies what she's made. She's just happy to have made the thing, and that happy is contagious. In a vast sea of stunning DIY-focused blogs with shiny photographs portraying impossible lifestyles, Jasika's Instagrams of her projects-in-progress provide some sweet relief. Unsurprisingly, she waxed the most philosophical of all the people I interviewed for this book. I was especially moved by her reply when I asked about her ugly voice, and she came right back with the assumption that there's an equal and opposite voice too.

"For me, duality is necessary. I can't have a voice in my head telling me that I am awesome all the time without a counter voice telling me that I suck. It's a part of life—pros and cons to everything, people who like you and people who don't, people who *you* like and people you don't, things that make you happy and things that make you sad. If there is a possibility that who you are is perfect, there also has to exist the possibility that you are imperfect. And maybe both of those things are true. Or maybe neither of them is true. The point is, doubt and worry and self-consciousness are integral parts of how we exist in the world, and I don't think we have to look at that 'ugly' voice as a bad thing—maybe that voice can provide some incentive for us, or force us into a having a different perspective, or just motivate us to prove it wrong. Sometimes the ugly voice can help shine light on what your real anxieties are when it comes to being an artist, so at the most basic level, it's not the ugly voice that holds you back, it's your fears that make themselves known by manifesting themselves into the ugly voice."

I'm going to just leave it at that.

Acknowledgments

This book would not exist if Diane Gilleland hadn't taken my casual question about a tiny hint of an idea and run with it straight to her agent. That Kate McKean then agreed to represent me is one of the shiniest joys of my life. Thank you, Diane and Kate, for your support and friendship, and for challenging me to always be clearer and do better.

Gary Luke and the team at Sasquatch Books are wonderful humans who love books. With precision and enthusiasm, they pushed me to sculpt and nudge this one into shape. Michelle Hope Anderson, Sarah Hanson, Haley Stocking, Lisa Hay, and Kate Reingold, especially—thank you for all you do. Kate Bingaman-Burt's illustrations make my heart—and this book—sing.

Big love to the various coffee shops of Vancouver's deep West Side, and to CBC Radio One. The Vancouver Public Library was, as were the libraries of my youth, a stalwart companion.

To my preschool friends: thank you for cheering me on as I wrote and as we undertook potty training—both seemed like impossible challenges at times, and both were eased by your support. To my beloved crafty friends from near and far, your enthusiasm for Mighty Ugly and your unflagging belief that I could pull this off kept me going when the going was tough, and make me smile the rest of the time. To my dearest family and friends: I love you. Thank you for keeping it weird with me.

And to Greg, who held down the fort when I was working at night and through the weekend, so very many nights and weekends; for listening to me read aloud; for your belief in me; and for giving the best hugs in the world. And to Owen: yes, Mama's book is all done now.

Meet the Interviewees

Throughout the book are anecdotes and quotes from fifteen people I interviewed about their creative demons. I asked them about times they were sure they'd succeed but failed, and about times they were sure they'd crash and burn but ended up nailing it. I asked them to tell me what their ugly voice says to them, and how they're able to quiet it. I asked them how they feel when they're stuck, and what they do about it.

I didn't choose these people because they're famous—for the most part, they aren't. And I didn't choose them because they've gotten rich or done particularly outrageous things. I chose them because I admire them and how they apply their creativity. Some of them I know personally; most I don't (yet). Some are artists; some are crafters; some make things on a grand scale; some make things on a smaller scale. Some do work not conventionally seen as creative (let's change that).

Some I planned to invite into this book from the very beginning, when I was doing the initial planning; some I asked on a whim after reading something they wrote or discovering their work after meeting them through a mutual friend. Some write blogs I've read for years and years; some write blogs I discovered while I was writing the book. In all cases, these folks are fascinating people, and I've learned a lot from them. I hope you've learned a lot from them. And I hope you'll keep in mind that they're all human beings who struggle with their fears and demons, just like you do.

Let's say hello.

ALLISON HOFFMAN is a crochet artist, designer, and author. She crochets amigurumi dolls of pop-culture icons that bear uncanny and spectacular likenesses to the actual people. I first learned of her when I heard about a doll she crocheted in the likeness of Conan O'Brien, which eventually led her to met Conan O'Brien. Allison's eye for detail is awesome to me, literally, and the book she wrote about making crocheted dolls is sitting on the pile of all the things I'm going to make when I'm done writing this book (now that the book is out, I'm sure you can stalk my Instagram or something for evidence of all the things). I admire Allison's eye for detail, her sense of whimsy and fun, and her ability to reach a huge audience with her small creations. Allison's first book is *AmiguruME: Make Cute Crochet People* (Lark Crafts, 2013). Look her up at www.craftyiscool.com.

ANN FRIEDMAN is a journalist. I started following her work online after she, along with many of the people she worked with, was fired from her job as executive editor of *GOOD* magazine. In the aftermath, she and the others banded together to make a magazine of their own—a one-issue wonder called *Tomorrow*. Since that project, Ann has established herself as a freelance journalist. When I asked her what she does for fun, Ann told me: "I make little charts and doodles and write in my journal. I go thrift shopping and sew/alter my finds. I send ol' fashioned snail mail and packages to friends. Sometimes I make friendship bracelets." I admire Ann's perspective on her work and on the rapidly changing worlds of journalism and publishing, her sense of humor, and her feminism. Look her up at www.annfriedman.com.

BETSY CROSS is a jewelry designer and retail shop co-owner. She's one of the few people to have elicited a fangirl moment from me—I loved her jewelry first; when I met her in person, I believe I squealed. I remain her biggest fan, and feel very grateful to call her a friend. Betsy is one of the most daring small businesspeople I know. Her melding of craftsmanship and business prowess is brilliant, as seen in her ability to continually design new pieces, market them, and sell them both through her own website and shop, as well as wholesale across North America. I admire Betsy's integrity, her style, her generosity, and her sense of humor. Look her up at www.betsyandiya.com.

BETZ WHITE is a sewing pattern designer and author. Like me, she's interested in the creative process, and she's a parent who works from home. We've been tweeting at each other for quite some time, and I asked to interview her because I was interested in learning more about her process. I admire Betz's generous spirit, the way she expresses her love of nature and craft through her creations, and the thoughtful way she approaches her work. Look her up at www.betzwhite.com.

FAYTHE LEVINE is an independent researcher and documentary film-maker. I met her in person when she came to Vancouver to screen her first film, *Handmade Nation*. She stayed at my house when we were strangers to each other, and seeing her again when she came back to town a few years later to screen her *Sign Painters* film was a true treat (both seeing her and the film she made with Sam Macon). For fun, Faythe enjoys "thrift-store shopping, cooking, letter-writing, and reading." I admire her ability to take a step back from things that fascinate her so she can study them and tell their story, and she's one of the most interesting and open people I've ever met. Also, she's really fun to go shopping with. Look her up at www.faythelevine.com.

JASIKA NICOLE is an actor and artist. We've never met but I did once spy her at a craft fair in Vancouver during the time she was here filming *Fringe* (you'd know her as the actor who played Astrid).

Jasika writes one of my favorite blogs; her unfettered enthusiasm for making stuff—and for learning how to do things she's never done before—is happy-making and inspiring. For fun, she told me, "I knit, quilt, sew, embroider, paint, build and refinish furniture, reupholster, and bake." I admire the way Jasika inspires me to make stuff even when I have no idea what I'm doing, and the thoughtful way she approaches her projects and the world in general. Also, when I sent her a note on Tumblr out of nowhere and insisted I was legit, she believed me. Look her up at www.jasikanicole.com.

JOEL WATSON is a cartoonist. He makes a geek web comic called *HijiNKS ENSUE* that has cracked me up for years. When Joel decided to try to make his living exclusively from the comic, he documented his trials and tribulations publicly in a project he called The Experiment. That kind of honesty always draws me in, and I was pleased as punch when Joel agreed to be a part of this book. In addition to his honesty, I admire his ability to combine his passion for geekery with a killer sense of humor through a medium I love. And once, I met him at Baltimore Comic-Con, but I haven't mentioned it to him because I'm sure he doesn't remember and I feel kind of dumb. Look him up at www.hijinksensue.com.

KATE BINGAMAN-BURT is an illustrator and educator who is also the person who illustrated this book. True story: I've loved Kate's work for many years, and almost fell out of my chair when I learned she would be illustrating *Mighty Ugly*. I've seen this whole thing as an opportunity to force myself to say hello to her, which I did, and then

I asked her a lot of questions about failure. You may have heard of Kate because for eight years she drew what she bought every day, and before that she drew her credit card statements every month until she got herself out of debt. She's my hero. Check out her books, *Obsessive Consumption: What Did You Buy Today?* (Princeton Architectural Press, 2010) and *What Did I Buy Today?: An Obsessive Consumption Journal* (Princeton Architectural Press, 2012), and look her up at www.katebingamanburt.com.

KIRSTY HALL is an artist and purveyor of mad obsessive projects. I was relieved when Kirsty said explicitly that she's obsessive in her art, because that obsession is what draws me to it, but I wasn't sure it would be OK to say that out loud. She does things like embark on a project to make art in a Mason jar every day for a year, hiding each jar in public along with instructions on how to alert her when the jar is found. It's that I'm so entirely different in the way I work that draws me to Kirsty, I think. I admire the small details and dogged determination she infuses her work with; it contrasts mightily with the spontaneity and broad strokes that define mine. Look her up at www.kirstyhall.co.uk.

LAUREN BACON is an author, tech entrepreneur, and business coach. Though I've read her outstanding blog for a long time, I asked her for an interview only a few weeks before my writing deadline after I read one of her posts on impostor syndrome. She graciously agreed to tell me more about her own experiences and how she works with her clients, most of whom are entrepreneurs. I admire her not only for her unflagging support of women in tech, but also her abilities to write about complex topics simply and clearly and to relate her own experiences in ways that are universally applicable. Look her up at www.laurenbacon.com.

NOAH SCALIN is an artist, author, designer, and activist. Perhaps you've heard of his Skull-A-Day project? His book *Unstuck* is an occasional savior of mine. Noah has a knack for making it feel totally normal and OK to hit snags. So much so that I will want to hug him if I'm lucky enough to meet him in person; that might be awkward but maybe it won't be. For fun, Noah sings in his band, League of Space Pirates, which is named after the science fiction universe he plays in. I admire Noah for enthusiastically pursuing a variety of seemingly unrelated projects, and for encouraging (and helping) people to do their thing. Look him up at www.noahscalin.com.

RACHAEL ASHE is an artist and maker whose creations in paper rarely fail to blow my mind. We've been friends for several years, and our infrequent coffee dates to catch up about our respective projects are always a highlight of my workday. Also, she knows where to get the best pastries in town. It was when Rachael delivered a Creative Mornings Vancouver talk about her evolution as an artist that I knew I had to interview her. She advocated creating a whole lot of crappy work and making lots of mistakes—I mean, right? Look her up at www.portfolio.rachaelashe.com.

RACHAEL HERRON is a writer. I've read her knitting blog for many, many years, and so I've also watched the evolution of her writing career, from hobbyist to published author of several novels and a memoir. For her day job, Rachael works as a 911 dispatcher; her melding of these two very different careers fascinates me. I was thrilled when Rachael agreed to be part of this book not only because I'm a fan, but because she inspires me to make time for the things and people I love, and because I admire the honesty with which she discusses her work, her life, and her craft. Look her up at www.yarnagogo.com.

SONYA PHILIP is an artist who challenged herself to sew one hundred dresses in a year. Though I knew of that "100 Acts of Sewing" project, I didn't actually know Sonya until I tweeted one day that I was feeling desperate to learn how to sew clothes, and she humbly pointed me to a beginner dress pattern she was selling. I bought it, and asked her for an interview. I admire Sonya's passion for fiber art; her thoughtful exploration of art and craft, making and consuming; and her encouragement of all people to make. Look her up at www.sonyaphilip.com.

STACEY ROZICH is an artist and illustrator. I first met her on the side of the road; she was an unexpected third passenger, joining Faythe Levine and her filmmaker partner Sam Macon in my cramped car when I drove them across Vancouver for the screening of the *Sign Painters Movie*. So I fell in love with Stacey before I discovered she's an artist, and then I fell in love with her art. I went down a Google rabbit hole, and knew I needed to ask my new friend to join me on this book adventure. She graciously obliged, and I hope she's not creeped out that I want us to be friends for life. I admire Stacey's exploration of folklore and scary figures in her art, her passion for research, and her thoughtful perspective on her own art and career. Look her up at www.staceyrozich.com.

For Further Exploration

BOOKS

* *344 Questions: The Creative Person's Do-It-Yourself Guide to Insight, Survival, and Artistic Fulfillment*, by Stefan G. Bucher

* *The Antidote: Happiness for People Who Can't Stand Positive Thinking*, by Oliver Burkeman

* *The Beauty of Different: Observations of a Confident Misfit*, by Karen Walrond

* *Creative Confidence: Unleashing the Creative Potential Within Us All*, by Tom Kelley and David Kelley (Crown Business, 2013)

* *The Creative Habit: Learn It and Use It for Life*, by Twyla Tharp

* *The Collaborative Habit: Life Lessons for Working Together*, by Twyla Tharp

* *Creative Block: Get Unstuck, Discover New Ideas. Advice & Projects from 50 Successful Artists*, by Danielle Krysa

* *Creative You*, by David B. Goldstein and Otto Kroeger

* *Ignore Everybody: And 39 Other Keys to Creativity*, by Hugh MacLeod

* *The Inner Game of Tennis: The Classic Guide to the Mental Side of Peak Performance*, by W. Timothy Gallwey

* *Neil Gaiman's "Make Good Art" Speech*, by Neil Gaiman, illustrated by Chip Kidd

* *On Writing*, by Stephen King

* *The Pocket Scavenger*, by Keri Smith

* *The Power of Habit: Why We Do What We Do in Life and Business*, by Charles Duhigg

* *Show Your Work!: 10 Ways to Share Your Creativity and Get Discovered*, by Austin Kleon

* *Steal Like an Artist: 10 Things Nobody Told You About Being Creative,* by Austin Kleon
* *The Universal Traveler: A Soft-Systems guide to creativity, problem-solving and the process of reaching goals,* by Don Koberg and Jim Bagnall
* *Unstuck: 52 Ways to Get (and Keep) Your Creativity Flowing at Home, at Work and in Your Studio,* by Noah Scalin
* *The War of Art: Break Through the Blocks and Win Your Inner Creative Battles,* by Steven Pressfield

RADIO AND PODCASTS

* *Q, This American Life, Fresh Air, Radiolab, Welcome to Night Vale*

RECOMMENDATIONS AND REFERENCES FROM THE OTHER VOICES IN THIS BOOK:

ALLISON HOFFMAN: "My favorite things to read to get inspired are craft anthologies and home decorating books from the 1950s, '60s and '70s, like *Good Housekeeping New Complete Book of Needlecraft.* I love the vintage aesthetic that you can absorb by going through these books. Movies and TV definitely feed my creativity. I always turn to shows I loved growing up when I start thinking of new stuff to make."

ANN FRIEDMAN: "I have found Susan Sontag's journals to be incredibly inspirational. When I was reading both the first and second volumes, I felt a real surge of creativity in my own work. I think something about reading the unedited, not-meant-for-publication thoughts of such a great writer opened up new creative pathways for me."

BETSY CROSS: "I like reading books about the way other cultures create and the evolution of that throughout history. I like reading about indigenous art and craft practices. I also like to focus on a different art medium to find inspiration."

BETZ WHITE: "[I love] *The Universal Traveler!* I love looking at all kinds of craft and design books and books about the work of different artists, designers, and inventors in history."

FAYTHE LEVINE: "I love biographies and autobiographies about amazing, wild people. Most photography books, but specifically the 1960s to '80s photojournalism. I love all Roald Dahl and also am a huge fan of young adult fiction from the 1960s through the early '80s, when stories were still dark, complicated, and grim."

JASIKA NICOLE: "All how-to books! Even the ones that explain how to do things I don't care to learn about are pretty fascinating to me. I like big pictures and lots of clear directions typed underneath them."

JOEL WATSON: "When I'm writing I like to listen to music, but it has to be instrumental or I will focus too much on the words and won't be able to come up with my own. I like Zoe Keating (instrumental cello), and a lot of instrumental prog-metal (Chimp Spanner, Cloudkicker) when I'm writing. Once I'm drawing, I'll usually put my entire iTunes playlist on random or listen to a comedy podcast (*Comedy Bang Bang, Doug Loves Movies, How Did This Get Made, The Pod F. Tomkast*). Anything that entertains without asking me to look up from my work."

KIRSTY HALL: "I have four creativity books that I return to time and again: *Art & Fear* by David Bayles and Ted Orland, *Everyday Sacred* by Sue Bender, *The Creative Habit* by Twyla Tharp, *Creating A Life Worth Living* by Carol Lloyd (this is a career advice book for us 'square peg' types, and it was truly radical for me when I was searching for a meaningful way to be in the world). I love reading non-fiction, especially history books. I'm a sucker for those 'history and cultural meanings of a commodity'–type books such as *Salt: A World History* by Mark Kurlansky, or *Color: Travels Through the Paintbox* by Victoria Finlay. Inspiration comes from odd places. For example, my knotted sculpture, '3 Score & 10,' was inspired by the lovely knot illustrations at the start of every chapter in Annie Proulx's novel *The Shipping News*."

LAUREN BACON: "I recommend Twyla Tharp's *The Creative Habit* to everyone. And Stephen Pressfield's *The War of Art*, the podcast *Creative Little Beasts* by Danielle Maveal, and pinterest.com, daniellelaporte.com, taramohr.com, heartofbusiness.com."

NOAH SCALIN: "I grew up on the Susan Striker's Anti-Coloring Books (bit.ly/anticoloring), and I'm so happy that they're still around for kids (and adults) today! I've actually found the business book *Good To Great* by Jim Collins to be a constant inspiration. It's not aimed at creative people, but the lessons definitely apply. I'm also in a book club and read something new and interesting every month. I love reading things that aren't directly related to whatever I'm doing in my life at the moment; inevitably, I'll find something in them that inspires creative endeavors down the line. My brain definitely thrives on audio input. I'm a music addict, but I also subscribe to a ton of podcasts (including *Radiolab, This American Life, Studio 360, Bullseye,* and *The Accidental Creative*)."

RACHAEL ASHE: "Because I've been focused on learning more about paper and book art these last few years, I've collected books on these subjects. I often look through these when I need ideas or inspiration. A few of my favorites: *Paper Works*, published by Ginko Press; *Paper-Craft 2: Design and Art with Paper*, published by Gestalten; *Irving Harper, Works In Paper*, edited by Michael Maharam."

RACHAEL HERRON: "Stephen King's *On Writing* is one of the best books out there (yes, that Stephen King). Anne Lamott's *Bird by Bird* also talks a lot about self-doubt and how to work in spite of it. Podcasts are great. I find hearing stories about other people's lives sparks ideas in my mind—that wonderful moment of wondering 'what if?' *This American Life* is my favorite. I save the episodes up and listen to them while knitting or sewing."

SONYA PHILIP: "*100 Demons* by Lynda Barry is a great one. So is *Steal Like an Artist* by Austin Kleon. I love old botanical and scientific drawings, so Albert Seba's *Natural Curiosities* is a treasure trove. At the end of the day, I like to trawl around tumblr.com or pinterest.com, looking at the images. I also love rewatching movies, like anything by Wes Anderson, and period dramas like *Bright Star* or *Vanity Fair*."

STACEY ROZICH: "Most of my book collection is devoted to books that inspire this strange combustion engine that is my imagination. They range from world folk art, masks of Mexico, ancient and contemporary textiles, American quilts, traditional folk costumes of Central Europe, West African craft tradition, eighteenth-century biological lithographs, and the list goes on."

About the Author

KIM PIPER WERKER is a writer and freelance editor who tries to make something—anything—every day. Many of those things are awful; some are not. Originally from Brooklyn, NY, she lives in Vancouver, BC. Learn more about her work, teaching schedule, and rag-tag adventures at KimWerker.com. For more on Mighty Ugly, including links to resources and a book-club guide, visit MightyUgly.com.

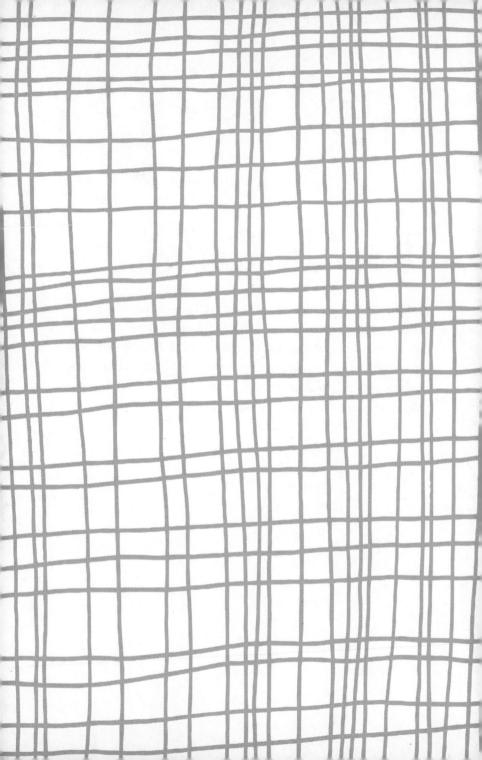